# THE NORTH YORK MOORS

## MOORS

### NATIONAL PARK

# THE NORTH YORK MOORS
## NATIONAL PARK

Ian Carstairs

*Webb & Bower*
MICHAEL JOSEPH

## Acknowledgements

Special thanks to Don Spratt, Alan Staniforth, Richard Groom and Janet Knoulson for helpful advice in the preparation of the text.

Photographic credits: photographs by Ian Carstairs, the North York Moors National Park and the Yorkshire and Humberside Tourist Board; additional new photographs taken for the Countryside Commission by Charles Meecham. Special thanks are due to the following for photographs: National Remote Sensing Centre, p 7; the town of Bayeux, p 61 and the Victoria & Albert Museum, p 72.

First published in Great Britain 1987 by
Webb & Bower (Publishers) Limited
9 Colleton Crescent, Exeter, Devon EX2 4BY
in association with Michael Joseph Limited
27 Wright's Lane, London W8 5SL
and The Countryside Commission,
John Dower House, Crescent Place,
Cheltenham, Glos GL50 3RA

Designed by Ron Pickless

Production by Nick Facer/Rob Kendrew

Illustrations by Rosamund Gendle/Ralph Stobart

Text and new photographs Copyright © The Countryside Commission
Illustrations Copyright © Webb & Bower (Publishers) Ltd

### British Library Cataloguing in Publication Data
The National parks of Britain.
North Yorkshire Moors
1.  National parks and reserves — England —
Guide-books   2.   England — Description and
travel — 1971–    — Guide-books.
I.   Carstairs, Ian
914.2′04858   SB484.G7.

ISBN 0–86350–140–0

Typeset in Great Britain by Keyspools Ltd., Golborne, Lancs.

Printed and bound in Hong Kong by Mandarin Offset

# Contents

# Preface

The North York Moors is one of ten national parks which were established in the 1950s. These largely upland and coastal areas represent the finest landscapes in England and Wales and present us all with opportunities to savour breathtaking scenery, to take part in invigorating outdoor activities, to experience rural community life, and most importantly, to relax in peaceful surroundings.

The designation of national parks is the product of those who had the vision, more than fifty years ago, to see that ways were found to ensure that the best of our countryside should be recognized and protected, that the way of life therein should be sustained, and that public access for open-air recreation should be encouraged.

As the government planned Britain's post-war reconstruction, John Dower, architect, rambler and national park enthusiast, was asked to report on how the national park ideal adopted in other countries could work for England and Wales. An important consideration was the ownership of land within the parks. Unlike other countries where large tracts of land are in public ownership, and thus national parks can be owned by the nation, here in Britain most of the land within the national parks was, and still is, privately owned. John Dower's report was published in 1945 and its recommendations accepted. Two years later another report drafted by a committee chaired by Sir Arthur Hobhouse proposed an administrative system for the parks, and this was embodied in the National Parks and Access to the Countryside Act 1949.

This Act set up the National Parks Commission to designate national parks and advise on their administration. In 1968 the National Parks Commission became the Countryside Commission but we continue to have national responsibility for our national parks which are administered by local government, either through committees of the county councils or independent planning boards.

This guide to the landscape, settlements and natural history of the North York Moors National Park is one of a series on all ten parks. As well as helping the visitor appreciate the park and its attractions, the guides outline the achievements and pressures facing the national park authorities today.

Our national parks are a vital asset, and we all have a duty to care for and conserve them. Learning about the parks and their value to us all is a crucial step in creating more awareness of the importance of the national parks so that each of us can play our part in seeing that they are protected for all to enjoy.

Sir Derek Barber
Chairman
Countryside Commission

# Introduction

On an infra-red photograph taken from space the North York Moors stands out clearly, tucked against the coast beneath the Tees estuary and isolated from the Pennines by the Vale of York.

The colours in the photograph are not the true colours of the land. They are the result of the particular photographic technique used. Each shade represents a different type of vegetation and from the distribution of individual colours the pattern of land use can be worked out. The sea is deep purple, the farming valleys red and the extensive urban and industrial areas of Middlesbrough and Teesside mid blue. In the centre it is bottle green. This is heather moorland.

Heather holds a special place in the hearts of millions. It is a romantic symbol associated with good luck, and few holiday-makers return from

Infra-red photograph taken from space.

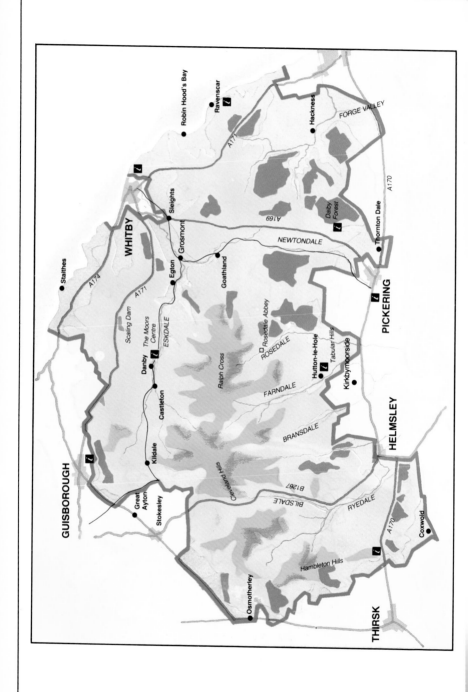

places where it is in bloom without at least a small sprig wedged somewhere on the front of the car. But maybe there is a bit more to it than that. Perhaps they are also saying to everyone, 'Look!, I have been to wild and remote places', for that is the very nature of the landscapes where heather grows.

In 1952, 553 square miles of the North York Moors were designated as a national park, principally to conserve the heather moorland, though it also encompassed numerous areas of traditional farmland, conifer forests and ancient deciduous woodland, as well as twenty-five miles of rugged coast.

This is the only national park in the east. Snowdonia, Pembrokeshire Coast and Brecon Beacons all lie in Wales; Dartmoor and Exmoor in the south west; the Lake District in the north west; and Northumberland, the Yorkshire Dales and the Peak straddle the Pennines in a vertical line down the centre of England.

The moors look totally different depending from where they are viewed. Seen across the Vale of Pickering from the Howardian Hills or Yorkshire Wolds, they rise as a long, low hump on the horizon. In stark contrast, from Stokesley the Cleveland Hills escarpment forms a steep mountain backdrop. From the east, a view rarely enjoyed by the visitor, they offer an abrupt wall of high cliffs to the North Sea: the loftiest, Boulby Head at 660 ft (201 m) is the highest sea cliff in eastern England. From the coast this great slab of land, etched by deep valleys, stretches inland as it rises gradually to nearly 1,500 ft (460 m) on Urra Moor.

The North York Moors have many faces, but the most enduring image of all is undoubtedly from within the high moors themselves. It is a classic experience to stand on the tops above Farndale or Rosedale in springtime and to gaze over the treeless ridges, which fade one by one to the distant horizon. Below lie the dazzling greens of new grass in the farming valleys and above the wide sweep of the sky where the call of the curlew is carried on the wind.

There are few landscapes in Britain so precisely defined by their natural boundaries. Along one side lies the sea and on the others the slopes of the upland block. The national park boundary follows roughly the same lines, although on the coast it cuts inland to skirt Whitby and Scarborough.

All told it is nearly 150 miles around the perimeter of the national park. Britain may be an overcrowded

The moorlands of the North York Moors form the largest tract of continuous heather in England and Wales.

*Facing* The North York Moors National Park.

island, but there is no shortage of space in this region: just 25,000 people live here. Much of the population is thinly spread in isolated farmsteads, and there are no large towns. Only Staithes and Robin Hood's Bay on the coast, Thornton Dale and Helmsley in the south, Osmotherley in the west and a string of several villages in the Esk Valley reach an appreciable size.

Until 1974 the whole of the North York Moors lay within the North Riding of Yorkshire. Following local government reorganization the majority fell within the new county of North Yorkshire and the remainder, about four per cent, into another new county, Cleveland.

In these uplands modern society has been fortuitously restrained in its effects on the countryside. It has not consumed the evidence of the lives of our ancestors, nor obliterated the marks of the hand of nature. Life up here is hard, the soil generally poor and the weather often harsh. With vast areas of heather still managed traditionally for grouse and sheep the pace of change is slow. These are the characteristics which have helped to preserve the details of the landscape to delight the visitor. Bronze Age burial mounds and field cairns still dot the moorlands in their thousands; and ruined abbeys, ancient crosses and the derelict remains of bygone industries all add their testimony to the history of the scene. Amidst all this there is a variety of wildlife now so noticeably lacking in most of lowland Britain.

On the coast, itself specially defined as a heritage coast, the sea which chewed the precipitous cliffs out of the upland block has exposed the rock strata in many places. Between Whitby and Scarborough geological history is presented in an open-air textbook of national importance. No-one can fail to be moved by the awesome powers which manoeuvered these rocks to their present place, and within exposed rock-faces or on the beach after a storm the sharp-eyed may readily come across the fossilized remains of plants and animals which once lived here.

There are numerous qualities of the moors worthy of superlative description. However, these must be left for individuals to identify and express for themselves. But, if there is one quality which surely warrants special mention, it must be the overwhelming sense of freedom within these hills – even at the height of the busiest season the pressures of the world still seem very far away.

# 1 The roots of the moorland scenery

Look at the picture of Rievaulx Abbey. What do you see?

A magnificent ruin? Or a large number of carefully cut blocks, each one quarried from the surrounding hills?

Rocks matter. They are the very roots of the scenery with an influence far beyond the dry terminology of geological descriptions. Every single twist and fold of the land, human settlement, plant and animal has in some way a link with them, their shape or the soils they produce. The history of these invisible roots of the landscape is written in code across the entire face of the national park. If we can read the code, then the story of the rocks beneath the surface will immediately come alive.

Large numbers of visitors to the North York Moors enter the national park along the Thirsk to Helmsley road. About eight miles east of Thirsk, Whitestone Cliff rises sharply above the valley floor near where the road winds steeply up Sutton Bank. With the engine in low gear and revving hard, thousands of heavily laden cars struggle up this immense hill, notable for its boil-ups on hot summer days. But the climb is far more than a 300-foot ascent. It is also a journey through time, past rocks laid down on the bed of an ancient sea as sandy deposits which have been pushed and shoved by forces in the Earth's crust, lifted out of the sea and then assaulted by the erosive powers of the elements.

Sutton Bank Top on a clear day is an inspiring place to contemplate the history of the landscape. Beyond the Vale of York lie the Pennines; to the right Lake Gormire; to the left the conical Hood Hill and the sheer face of Roulston Scar with its airfield. How did this all happen? How long have people been here? How have they affected the landscape and how in turn has the landscape affected them?

Overhead, gliders manoeuvre to take advantage of the currents and thermals which sweep upwards from the escarpment, providing a direct example of the influence of the shape of the land: it is fair to say that they too are only here because of the rocks.

Rievaulx Abbey. Stone for the buildings was quarried nearby, then brought to the abbey site along a canal which the monks had made.

In clear weather it is possible to see more than ninety miles from the top of Sutton Bank.

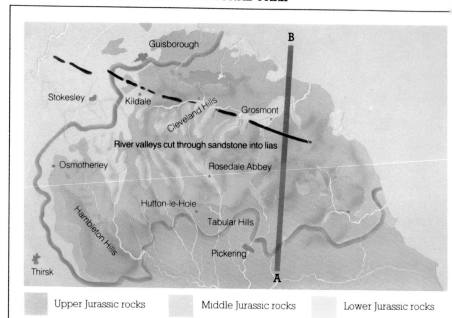

Upper Jurassic rocks     Middle Jurassic rocks     Lower Jurassic rocks

Park boundary     Cleveland Dyke

The North York Moors is, geologically, the youngest national park in England and Wales. Its visible landscape is formed from rocks a mere one-third the age of those of the Lake District.

Broadly speaking the evolution of the moors can be simplified into four basic types of geological activity – sedimentation, folding, uplift, and erosion.

At the dawn of Jurassic times – 210 million years ago – the whole area lay under a deep sea. Sediments deposited slowly on the bed of this sea were ultimately compressed to form the Lias – grey shales – which underlie the whole national park. There are three main divisions in the Lias: the Lower, Middle and Upper. These Liassic rocks were then folded, and following a period of erosion, covered by further deposits, as the Dogger – an iron rich sandstone – was laid down.

By the Middle Jurassic age major changes had occurred. Instead of the sea a huge delta, fed by rivers from Scandinavia, now spilled across the region. In this halfway world between land and water, freshwater muds, sands and silts – the origins of the massive moorland sandstone – were deposited. Slight changes in sea level or the height of the land could tip the scales in favour of one or the other. On four occasions the sea submerged the delta to varying extents. The first three times the

Geological map of
The North York Moors

*Facing* geological section

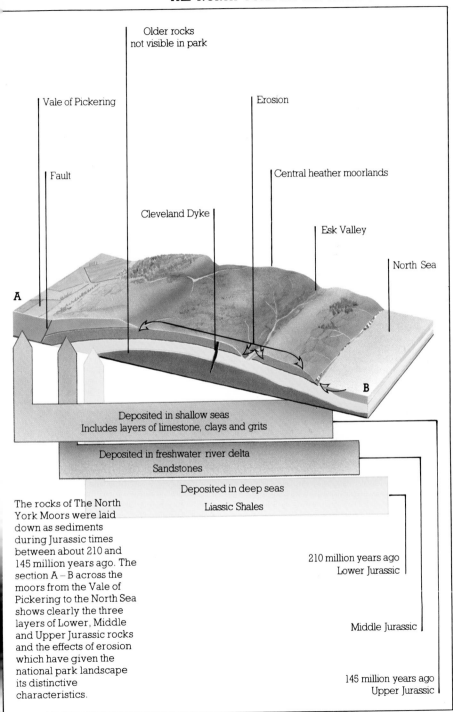

Older rocks
not visible in park

Vale of Pickering

Erosion

Fault

Central heather moorlands

Cleveland Dyke

Esk Valley

North Sea

A

B

Deposited in shallow seas
Includes layers of limestone, clays and grits

Deposited in freshwater river delta
Sandstones

Deposited in deep seas
Liassic Shales

The rocks of The North York Moors were laid down as sediments during Jurassic times between about 210 and 145 million years ago. The section A – B across the moors from the Vale of Pickering to the North Sea shows clearly the three layers of Lower, Middle and Upper Jurassic rocks and the effects of erosion which have given the national park landscape its distinctive characteristics.

210 million years ago
Lower Jurassic

Middle Jurassic

145 million years ago
Upper Jurassic

delta recovered, each inundation being clearly marked by a seam of marine deposits. However, the fourth time it did not and the land remained under the sea.

In comparison with the marine conditions of the Lower Jurassic, the post-deltaic seas of the Upper Jurassic were relatively shallow and their sediments markedly different. Instead of substantial Liassic shales with thinner limestones and ironstones, they produced mainly limestones and sandstones, culminating in a thick layer of Kimmeridge clay.

A period of uplift and erosion then interrupted deposition, until about 145 million years ago. With the region still under water the Cretaceous period superseded the Jurassic and thick beds of chalk – the remains of myriads of sea creatures – were added to earlier layers.

Another huge gap in our geological knowledge followed, until between sixty and thirty million years ago, when the area felt the side effects of powerful activity a thousand miles away. In central Europe the Alps were being formed. Great forces were twisting and buckling the Earth's crust. The rocks here buckled too, though to a far lesser extent. As they folded, domes and basins developed in the strata and a number of faults occurred, principally on the coast and across the south of the national park.

In the same period, about fifty-eight million years ago, the only volcanic rocks squeezed through the strata in a narrow vertical band less than thirty-five feet wide. The Cleveland Dyke, or Whinstone Ridge, emerges near Great Ayton to run south east, before petering out at Blea Hill on Fylingdales Moor.

In late Tertiary times (which followed the Cretaceous period) extensive marine erosion planed the folded rocks flat. Then gradually, by movement in the Earth's crust, the surface was uplifted from under the water to form a long, gently sloping wedge of land extending from the Pennines to the sea.

To begin with, Pennine rivers flowed due east across the wedge. But variations in the contours and rates of erosion gradually altered their direction. Water draining radially from the Cleveland Dome – roughly where Ralph Cross stands today – was also deflected slightly east by the general tilt of the land, resulting in a 'herringbone pattern' of valleys leading north and south across the park.

Most of the dales were formed in a similar way. Initially streams cut steep 'V'-shaped valleys. But as

The Wainstones. A rocky outcrop resulting from water erosion.

the water wore deeper through the sandstones and into the Lias, spring erosion, known as sapping, joined in at the horizon between the two, greatly accelerating the sideways erosion. This broadened the valleys from a 'V' into a much wider and, in places, craggy shouldered 'U'. High on a ridge above Great Broughton, the rapid erosion which scooped out the boundary of the Cleveland Hills created the Wainstones, a curiously stacked and tumbled sandstone outcrop.

Simultaneously streams and rivers in the Pennines were cutting their own valleys. Eventually, by river capture, the cumulative effects, further influenced by later Ice Ages, diverted the eastwards flow of the main Pennine rivers down the Vale of York where the River Ouse runs today. In this way the North York Moors became a separate block, isolated largely by the erosive power of water, though assisted in part by ice and wind.

Erosion was by no means confined to valleys. All the while the sea pounded at the cliffs and the elements gradually stripped the softer overlying rocks from the moor tops.

The main heather moorland comprises sandstones of the Middle Jurassic, covered across the south of the park by the Upper Jurassic limestones of the Tabular Hills. These hills, aptly named for their table-like tops – the effect of intensive erosion on the flat strata in late Tertiary times – stretch in a prominent line of 'nabs' from

The north-facing slopes of the Tabular Hills continue to erode slowly southwards.

Scarborough to Black Hambleton thirty miles to the west. In the past these rocks, along with other younger layers, once covered the entire area. But progressive erosion has 'peeled' them back southwards from the domed centre of the moors. The Cretaceous chalks and younger Jurassic layers have gone completely, eroded beyond the park to the Wolds and Vale of Pickering respectively. Meanwhile the Tabular Hills continue to wear away. At Crosscliff viewpoint, Surprise View Gillamoor, Saltergate Bank and numerous other vantage points which lie on the frontier of the erosion, the vista graphically displays the retreating north-facing escarpment of the hills.

The same 'peeling back' also happened in a northwards direction away from the highest central ridge. Here it has been more complete. Only a strip of Kellaways rock now remains on the moortops around Danby Beacon.

Verification of this vast erosion of overlying layers lies on the hilltops to the north and south of Staindale. On the open moor and amidst the conifer forest the Bridestones and Adderstone – wind sculptured, top heavy remnants – jut somewhat forlornly above the surrounding ground.

The shaping of the North York Moors did not happen just in the past. It is still happening today. Every rain and snow storm, every frosty night and gale at sea, and every rock fall on the valley sides takes its toll. Hold your hand in a moorland stream and catch a few particles as they are washed down. This is geology in action.

Now that we have a 'feel' for the origins of the landscape it will be easier to interpret the influence of rocks in the everyday scene.

# 2 **Understanding the geology**

The national park coast is a Mecca for the study of geology. Between Boulby and Scarborough a wide range of strata, with their attendant fossils, faults and detailed geological features are ranked up from the foreshore to the clifftops in dramatic order. Nowhere can all the layers be seen in one place, though Robin Hood's Bay and Ravenscar display the widest and most accessible range.

From Ravenscar, at low tides, the striking effect of the wave-cut platform across Robin Hood's Bay dome leaves little doubt about its influence on the shape of the coast. Like a slice through a huge half-submerged onion, the concentric curves reveal where the softer layers of Lower Lias, the oldest visible rocks of the park, have eroded at a faster rate than the numerous bands of harder limestones and ironstones between them. Similarly, though less pronounced, eroded domes have influenced the coastline at Kettleness and Boulby to the north west of Whitby.

The word Lias comes from the Gaelic *leac* – a flat stone – an appropriate description for these layered

Low tide in Robin Hood's Bay reveals the curved layers of the eroded Robin Hood's Bay dome.

grey shales. All contain large numbers of fossils. Ammonites, belemnites, shellfish and gastropods (snails) are most common and at North Cheek extensive shell beds cover many square yards. Sometimes rarer fish and occasionally remains of the ichthyosaurus, a predatory marine reptile, have been found.

Ichthyosaurus.

Conditions in the deep seas of the early Jurassic were ideal for formation of fossils. When marine animals died their bodies fell to the sea bed. Softer parts decayed, but the harder shells or skeletons became fossilized in the still, compacted muds.

Ammonites were soft bodied, tentacled animals which lived in a coiled shell. They varied considerably in size, from a mere pin-head to as much as two feet in diameter. In the Whitby area, where they are known as 'snakestones', legend has it that St Hilda, prioress of an early Whitby Abbey, suffered badly from a plague of snakes. To rid herself of the nuisance she chopped off their heads and threw their bodies over the cliff, whence they promptly curled up and turned to stone.

The environment in the delta where the sandstones were laid down was much less suitable for the formation of fossils. In this turbulent world swirling currents and eddies continually disturbed the sands and silts. Nevertheless in the stiller parts evidence of plant and animal life has survived: even the ripple marks made by water on the mudbanks have been detected in fossil form. Shellfish are occasionally found and at Gristhorpe, Cloughton and Whitby, plant beds contain numerous remains.

When plants became embedded in the muds chemical changes converted them to carbon. Substantial accumulations of plant material washed from the delta gave rise to moorland coal seams, whereas individual specimens formed finely detailed sooty imprints in the rock.

Prehistoric times inevitably conjure images of dinosaurs. While no remains of land animals have been discovered we know they were here. As dinosaurs moved over the soft sand banks they left footprints behind. In certain conditions, perhaps as the mud baked dry, prints were preserved as if the animal had passed by this way only yesterday.

Plant fossils make sooty imprints in the rock.

Most of the fossilized species of plants and animals found in the North York Moors have been extinct for tens of millions of years. Yet some animals, such as whelks, scallops and razor-fish and plants resembling maidenhair tree and horsetails have remained virtually unchanged to this day. It is therefore a sobering thought that the 'marestail' which tests a gardener's patience to extremes has direct links with plants of those primeval swamps.

At Ravenscar the Peak Fault marks a sudden downward displacement of the strata by several hundred feet. Immediately to the north the cliffs are dominated by the Lias, to the south sandstones drop in a single step to the sea.

It is tempting to imagine the land simply slumped, but this was not the case. Variation in the levels of strata occurred when the land fractured and the two blocks slid alongside each other. With uneven folds and thicknesses of individual layers, once they had moved the strata no longer matched up.

Between Ravenscar and Cloughton sandstones produce a more uniform coastline than the multi-layered and softer Lias from Boulby to Robin Hood's Bay. At Hundale Point massive beds with intermediate marine deposits show clearly the inundations of the Middle Jurassic delta by the sea.

The resistance of different strata to erosion can play as important a part in shaping the land as the power of erosion itself.

At Ravenscar, on a small scale, patches of resistant limestone in the Lias protect softer shales below, leaving 'mermaid's tables' isolated on the shore. At the other end of the scale some coastal towns and villages such as Robin Hood's Bay and Scarborough and Filey to the south of the park developed in the lea of more resistant headlands, which sheltered the town and harbour from the prevailing storms. Without different rates of erosion there would have been no Scarborough Castle Hill, no Scarborough Castle and perhaps no Scarborough either.

Erosion by streams and springs is far less dynamic than erosion by the sea, but the ultimate effects are equally dramatic.

The Hole of Horcum, a huge natural amphitheatre, lies beside the Pickering to Whitby road near the summit of the Tabular Hills at Saltergate. Folklore attributes its origin to anti-social behaviour by one Wade, a mythical giant of these parts who, in a fit of temper, reputedly picked up a great lump of ground and hurled it at his wife. He missed, but the result was the simultaneous creation of the Hole of Horcum and Blakey Topping, a symmetrical hill one and a half miles away.

The true origins of both are rather less colourful and a good deal less instantaneous. Extensive spring-sapping cut the Hole of Horcum in a natural

The Hole of Horcum – a vast natural amphitheatre beside the Pickering to Whitby road.

depression of the strata, and Blakey Topping is simply an outlier of clay protected by a cap of resistant sandstone left when its surroundings eroded away. Similar outliers occur at Freeborough Hill, near the Whitby to Guisborough road north of Castleton; Howden Hill near Hackness; and the best known hill in the national park, Roseberry Topping, near Great Ayton. Roseberry had a further impact on its looks in the nineteenth century when undermining for ironstone caused the whole west face to collapse.

It is difficult to believe the North York Moors has possibly been the most mined national park in England and Wales. Deposits of alum – used as a fix in the dyeing trade – and jet – a fossilized conifer – occur in the Lias; iron in the Lias and Dogger; coal among the sandstones; and potash – a fertilizer and the only deposit still mined – lies in the Permian rocks far below the surface.

Where these have been exploited over the centuries signs of mining activity provide as clear an indication of the nature of the rocks as if the whole strata was open to view.

Alum and iron mining had the most profound effects on the environment. Extraction of alum shale along the coast from Kettleness to Ravenscar near Guisborough and at Carlton Bank demolished local landscapes, both through quarrying and the tipping of tell-tale pink spoil.

Jet lies just below alum in the Upper Lias. Where these thin and sporadic deposits were easily accessible, such as in Scugdale, abandoned workings form a definite line of small spoil-heaps around the valley side.

Although iron had been worked since prehistoric

Scarborough harbour and waterfront are sheltered from North Sea storms by the promontory of Scarborough Castle Hill.

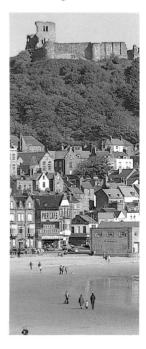

The site of Rosedale East mines entrance today. Little is left to testify to the hive of industry which once filled the valley.

times, mining only began in earnest when substantial ores were discovered in the Middle Lias during construction of a railway tunnel at Grosmont in 1835. More mines worked the seams in Glaisdale, but it is in Rosedale that the greatest evidence of past iron industry can still be seen. In the 1800s extensive mining of the Dogger ironstone blighted the valley. These wounds have not healed. They have, however, mellowed and today industrial archaeological remains of kilns and abandoned railtracks make a fascinating contribution to the character of the dale. In our conservation conscious world they provide considerable food for thought. Who now would tolerate the mess here of 100 years ago? Yet it is the legacy of that very mess from which we can now derive pleasure and historical interest.

Add to all this the mining of moor coal and quarrying for building materials, and the importance of rocks takes on more dimensions. Moor pits dot the uplands, and local rocks – limestones in the south and sandstones to the north – are reflected in buildings throughout the park, from village houses to mighty monastic ruins.

Man's opportunism is unceasing; even the narrow whinstone ridge has been quarried and mined as a roadstone. There are gas and oil deposits beneath the North York Moors. It will be interesting to see, in the light of history, how restrained our society is prepared to be with their extraction, or conversely how sensitively these resources can be used without damaging the countryside.

# 3 **The Ice Age**

Ninety thousand years ago at the onset of the last Ice Age – there have been at least four over the last two million years – the shape of the moors landscape looked much as it does today. In northern Britain glaciers developed in the mountains, and ice flowed eastwards from the Lake District and south from Scotland and Scandinavia. Unlike the penultimate Ice Age, during which ice completely covered the area, this time it was neither thick enough nor powerful enough to ride right over the top. Instead the Lake District ice divided. Part turned south down the Vale of York, while the remainder continued eastwards to unite with the flow from Scotland. Both were then deflected along the coast by the more substantial and powerful Scandinavian ice-stream.

The ice pushed as far as ten miles inland. In Eskdale it reached at least to Lealholm and in the Vale of Pickering – at that time an inlet from the sea – to Wykeham. The Vale of York ice blocked the other ends of the valleys past Ampleforth and Kildale, as well as plugging the outlets of western dales. Meanwhile the moortops, which remained clear, had become a world of permanent snow. Animals and plants were forced south, though seeds may well have lain dormant, locked in time, in the frozen ground.

Fog in the Vale of York, banked up against the moors on a snowy day, gives a strong impression of what the moors might have looked like during the Ice Age.

Newtondale gorge near
Levisham station.

When the thaw finally began about 15,000 years
ago, meltwater, encircled by the retreating ice on
all but the southern side, could not readily escape.
To the north of the central watershed, between the
higher ground and the coast, and along the edge of
the Vale of York, it built up behind ice-walls or cut
channels under and around its edge.

In the later stages meltwater filled Upper Eskdale
above an ice dam near the Lealholm moraine.
Eventually Lake Eskdale overflowed through the
lowest point in the surrounding hills into a lake at
Glaisdale, and from that into another near
Goathland. Between them, close to Key Green,
parallel channels may mark pauses in the retreat of
the ice where the effects of draining water were
concentrated for longer periods of time.

An attractive walk from
Newtondale Halt station
on the Moors rail line
winds through steep and
remote countryside to
Needle Point on the
shoulder of the gorge.

In turn the lake at Goathland overflowed, sending
a cascade to Fen Bog and on down Newtondale. The
torrent snaked along an existing valley, gouging a
deep gorge in just a decade or two. Rocks stripped
from the valley side then spewed in a huge fan of
gravel across the bed of Lake Pickering where the
water finally cleared the hills.

From Needle Point, on the edge of the gorge
above Newtondale Halt, the spirit of the violence
which wrought this 'Grand Canyon' still hangs
heavily in the air. The rock layers on the opposite
wall have a 'recently bitten' appearance and the
huge empty chasm where the water once roared
now almost generates a noise of its own.

South of Robin Hood's Bay similar things
happened, only on a much smaller scale. Meltwater
trapped by the coastal ice gathered in valleys
around Hackness, spilled out and sliced a miniature

Newtondale through Forge Valley in order also to reach Lake Pickering.

This vast expanse of water needed an outlet too. Six miles south of Malton it found one, cutting yet another gorge, this time at Kirkham in the eastern end of the Howardian Hills.

Before the Ice Age the River Derwent flowed directly to the coast, north of Scarborough. Afterwards, the effects of the ice, erosion of new channels and accumulation of glacial deposits permanently deflected it inland down Forge Valley to join the Ouse near Selby. However, a new 'sea cut' excavated between Hackness and Scalby by Sir George Cayley in 1804 once more locally united part of its flow with the sea.

These meltwater engravings mark many another scene. Along the coast numerous channels link the higher ground with the sea; Scarth Nick, which was a focal point for cattle drovers going into the moors, developed where it poured from the Cleveland Hills, and below Sutton Bank Lake Gormire formed in a blocked spillway at the edge of the Vale of York ice.

Throughout the Ice Age large quantities of water also remained frozen in the ground, binding the soils into one continuous lump. As the thaw progressed, a sludge of water, soil and other shattered materials went on the move, slipping from the moortops to give a uniform, gentle slope to some lower valley sides.

When the ice disappeared, finely ground material, gravel and boulders picked up on its way simply dropped where the ice once stood. Along the coast red-brown boulder clay smothered everything, masking the shape of the land and forcing streams and rivers to seek new routes to the sea, often some distance from their original course.

In Upper Eskdale the smooth-bottomed valley, once the bed of the glacial lake, switches to an undulating boulder-clay terrain below Lealholm moraine. The River Esk breaches the moraine in Crunkley Gill, a steep ravine, before winding along numerous gorges through glacial deposits to reach the sea at Whitby.

Erratics, rocks dropped by the ice and subsequently washed from the boulder-clay clifftops at Robin Hood's Bay, provide final proof of the origins of the ice-sheets. Boulders, some weighing many tons, and smaller rocks of granite from Shap, gneiss from Scotland and porphyry from Norway lie isolated on the shore.

An erratic, carried by the ice and dropped when it melted. Note the comparison in size with a camera placed at its base.

The hyena, which lived in the North York Moors before the last Ice Age.

Rocks are not the only remains of the Ice Age. In 1821 during quarrying at Kirkdale, just outside the park, workmen discovered a cave containing numerous animal bones and teeth. Dismissing them as remains of cattle, they threw large quantities into the river and more were carted away among quarried roadstone.

A local doctor, John Harrison, noticed the unusual fragments on a roadway. Tracing their source to Kirkdale Cave, a specialist, Dr Buckland from Oxford, then made an astonishing discovery. The bones and teeth came from a bewildering array of animals, including straight-tusked elephant, hippopotamus, giant deer, bison, rhinoceros, wolf, brown bear, lion and large numbers of hyena, which lived here before the last Ice Age.

Many of the species fell into two distinct groups. Those of a cold steppe and others from a warm, or even sub-tropical environment. Close inspection also revealed hundreds of encrusted hyena droppings. The cave, it would seem, had been a hyena den as long as 100,000 years ago, to which prey had been dragged and eaten.

A puzzle remained. The bones were covered by a layer of mud, attributed at the time to the Biblical Flood. In 1821 no-one knew about the Ice Age or Lake Pickering, the rising waters of which drowned the entrance.

Further quarrying destroyed much of the cave; there is now little to see, save a slit in the quarry face and the short, low and muddy inner cave. But it would be a miserable person indeed who could not find time to stand where the road fords Hodge Beck and imagine the sub-tropical waterside world the hyenas viewed from its entrance. There was no trace of man in Kirkdale Cave.

# 3 **Early man in the moors**

Prehistory is an immense jigsaw puzzle in which the edge pieces are in place, but most of the rest are missing. Recent research work, aimed at interpreting the cultures and life-styles of early man in the moors, has sought to bridge many gaps. By integrating detailed archaeological, geological and palaeoecological (prehistoric natural history) information, researchers have tried, with broad brush strokes, to paint a more complete picture of prehistoric society in the region. Inevitably the picture is blurred, but as new discoveries are made it will continue to become clearer, or even radically change. But no-one can ever expect to know the full truth. For the prehistoric story is far more than an inventory of flints, ditches and mounds. It is the complex evolution of real people, their domestic activity and a changing struggle for survival in the environment and societies of their own times.

About 13000 BC, in the wake of the ice, a heathland of grasses and sedges, intermingled with mugwort, sorrel, cowberry and juniper covered the region. Over the next 3–4,000 years the climate fluctuated, see-sawing between warmer, colder and wetter periods. Each time it altered, the vegetation changed. Open scrubby woodland of birch, hazel and some Scots pine succeeded the heath, only to

Prehistoric time chart.

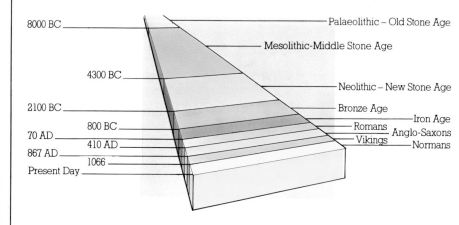

8000 BC ———————————————— Palaeolithic – Old Stone Age
———————— Mesolithic-Middle Stone Age
4300 BC ————
————————— Neolithic – New Stone Age
2100 BC ————
800 BC ———— Bronze Age
————— Iron Age
70 AD ———— Romans
410 AD ———— Anglo-Saxons
867 AD ———— Vikings
1066 ———— Normans
Present Day ————

revert, perhaps in a colder spell, then advance once more when the conditions warmed up again.

Following a considerable improvement in the climate 11,000 years ago, mixed deciduous woodland spread rapidly, though the higher and exposed locations probably remained as open woodlands with perhaps some oak and elm in sheltered places and heathland on the highest ground.

The moors were still virgin territory, responding only to the natural rhythms of the weather, plants and animals. This did not last long. Man was soon on the scene.

To the south Palaeolithic society was firmly established in Lincolnshire, Nottinghamshire and Derbyshire. With a low population and plentiful food supply to support a hunter/gatherer life-style no pressing need existed to develop new settlements further north, where it would have been, especially on the moors, colder and less hospitable. Nevertheless hunters occasionally came to the northern edge of the Vale of Pickering.

In a peat bog at Kildale Hall a window opened on the late Palaeolithic and early Mesolithic world when a local man, Roland Close, discovered the jumbled skeleton of an aurochs (wild ox), accompanied by a layer of charcoal. Some 10,000 years ago, when the aurochs may have died at the hands of a hunting party on a seasonal foray to the north, a swamp surrounded the site. Beyond that, a heathy grassland with open woods covered the immediate hills. This well suited the aurochs, wild horse, pig and red and roe deer which lived here. Indeed their browsing could well have helped to keep the vegetation open.

Mesolithic hunters visited the moors more frequently from about 8500 BC, possibly from the Vale of Pickering, where the edge of the marsh was occupied.

At the numerous hunting camps in the hills, flint nodules from the Yorkshire Wolds were worked into 'flint barbs' for weapons. With mean temperatures as much as seven degrees centigrade lower than today no-one lived here permanently. Even the hunting camps were probably only used in the short summer from about June to September.

Because larger numbers of animals inhabited open woodland than the clcsed forest, early man may have burned the vegetation to create new clearings and maintain existing open areas. The extra forest edge, greater variety of habitats and

abundant new shoots stimulated increases in the number of animals, many of which, especially deer, were attracted to the clearings, where they were more easily killed. In addition to meat, nuts, fruits and berries contributed to the diet. There was no shortage of these, particularly hazel nuts, in the regenerating shrubbery on the fired ground.

The Cleveland escarpment from Cook's Monument on Easby Moor.

Too much clearance in an area would have had the opposite effect. Beyond a critical point, the remaining woodland could no longer support the larger number of animals which the fire initially encouraged. In addition, with less cover, the larger species particularly were too easily caught by the hunters.

Early Mesolithic 'flint barbs' were bigger and more simply shaped than their later counterparts. Exactly what brought about this change is uncertain. Perhaps the style of weapons altered, or maybe different sized quarry was pursued – could it even be that Mesolithic man had already over-exploited the larger animals?

A price had to be paid for manipulating the forest. In the burnt areas soils began to erode, nutrients leached away and the loss of vegetation interrupted transpiration. Instead of being drawn up through plants, water lay in the ground and with a wetter climate blanket peat started to form. Although plants and trees grew again, degeneration of the upland soil had begun.

Late Mesolithic temperatures rose steadily until they became slightly higher than today's. Birch woodland developed into a Scots pine forest, followed in many areas by mixed oak woodland, although heath and grassland still clung on where forest failed to reach the highest ground.

Britain was totally populated by 5000 BC when Neolithic culture reached England from Europe. Offshoots from the major settlements in the Yorkshire Wolds moved into the North York Moors, across the Tabular Hills, into Lower Eskdale; on to the boulder clay along the coast and towards Teesside. It is no coincidence that the areas chosen reflect the distribution of good farming land – a feature which can be traced throughout history and prehistory.

The increasing population brought needs for change. No longer could a simple hunter/gatherer economy guarantee sufficient food. Cyclical woodland clearance continued and hunters still made seasonal trips up to the higher grounds but more intensive methods of land use and organized farming developed: some domestic stock now grazed the clearings and woodlands in the hills.

Prehistoric times are identified by the artefacts of their different cultures, though these did not change wholesale overnight. The old ways or technologies took time to die out or become absorbed and in some cases continued in parallel for many centuries.

Neolithic long barrows (burial mounds) constructed between 4300 and 3300 BC are the oldest man-made structures in the park, though their importance is not matched by their appearance. The best known of the handful of these visually insignificant mounds of stone and earth, at Kepwick, East Ayton Field and Scamridge, gave little away about contemporary life. Only a pile of bones lay beneath them. A chambered cairn on Great Ayton Moor proved rather more interesting. Excavations in the 1960s exposed a rectangular chamber, a passage entrance and signs of extensive burning in a pit. The more recent discovery of a Neolithic long cairn, beneath a later Bronze Age round barrow at Street Houses, near Lythe, has been even more revealing. The cairn had a concave timber façade at one end, a well preserved mortuary house and fragments of pottery. Radio-carbon dating places its construction right at the end of the Neolithic long barrow period, about 3500 BC.

Distinctive styles of pottery belonged to particular periods, cultures and burial rituals. Neolithic Grimston Ware and decorated Peterborough Ware have been found across the south of the park and later grooved ware from settlement sites, mostly in the Tabular Hills. A wide range of tools, including knives and chisels were used in farming areas, but on the high ground hunters carried only the implements essential to their task.

Beaker ware, beautifully decorated, well fired pots of one to two pints capacity, common in burial rituals on the Continent, is closely associated with the Bronze Age, though it is first known from the North York Moors in late Neolithic times. However, it was the widespread use of bronze for weapons, ornament and other goods from about 2100 BC that truly opened this period of prehistoric industrial revolution. The Bronze Age was *the* era of the region. Never since has the number of people using the high ground been so great. The traces of their life-style – thousands of burial mounds, tools, weapons, ditch systems, fields, pottery and occasional remnants of stone circles – are spread widely throughout the moors, offering considerable opportunities to understand and interpret Bronze Age society.

Settlement continued in the traditional agricultural areas, but seasonal movement to hunt the high ground gradually diminished and finally ceased. Instead communal territories, centred in the valleys and extending up to the watershed, had evolved. Ridges were obvious meeting points between people living in the valleys to either side and with the development of a more organized society formed the logical boundaries, frequently marked by lines of round barrows. Indeed many ridges still form present-day township boundaries. It is therefore possible, though not provable, that our present territorial arrangements have their roots in prehistoric times.

On the tops arable crop production began, grazing in clearings and woodlands intensified, and forest destruction increased with a vengeance. Radio-carbon dating linked to pollen analysis from peat bogs at various places on the moors shows major clearance occurred on both the low and high ground. Around Fen Bog, in Newtondale, the trees had certainly thinned by 1800 BC and at Wheeldale Gill some 200 years later. Pollen samples collected beneath two round barrows at Burton Howes, above Ingleby Greenhowe, provided further precise indications of the changing environment. The earliest had been built in a woodland clearing, whereas by the time its later neighbour was constructed the barrows stood in an area of open land.

Round barrows, also known as burial mounds,

A replica of a Napoleonic Wars signalling beacon surmounts a Bronze Age burial mound at Danby Beacon, one of the highest points in the park to the north of the Esk Valley.

tumuli or howes, are a particular hallmark of the Bronze Age. Built between 2700 and 1600 BC from earth, sand, turf and stone, or a variety of these materials, they varied considerably in size, from 15 ft (5 m) to 90 ft (30 m) wide and up to 9 ft (3 m) high.

The contents of excavated barrows are relatively similar – a burial or cremation, funeral pottery and occasionally a battleaxe or dagger – suggesting they mark the final resting place of individuals of roughly equal status, probably local headmen. Two exceptionally rich burials at Loose Howe, where a body lay in a coffin with a cover, an oak canoe and dagger, and at Swarth Howe, where an ornamental urn, flint spears, jet ornaments and an empty stone cist with a cupstone accompanied the interment, point perhaps to a social stratum even higher than that of the local leaders.

While archaeologists have managed to excavate carefully some round barrows, an even larger number have been plundered by grave robbers over the centuries with no record of their contents being kept. Depressions in their centres bear witness to these depredations of the past.

One barrow looks much the same as the next. The most memorable are therefore those occupying prominent positions or with an additional, well known feature or interesting name. Three Howes on the ridge behind Hutton-le-Hole top-out the sweep of hillside above the most popular tourist village of the park; Lilla Howe on Fylingdales Moor is adorned by a later cross; and one of the barrows at Danby Beacon is surmounted by a replica of a signalling beacon dating from the Napoleonic Wars. Near the eastern end of the Dalby forest drive, a pair of barrows straddles the road and nearby in Wykeham Forest, close to the footpath from Baxter's View, the deliciously named 'Three Tremblers' are hidden among trees. What or whom they are named after no-one is quite sure.

However, not all humps on the skyline are burial mounds. Throughout the moors spoil-heaps from small moorland coal pits are a similar shape and, at a distance, difficult to tell apart. Clear examples are the line of spoil-heaps along the ridge to the east of Clitherbeck near the Moors Centre at Danby, where at least one heap has a capped 100-foot shaft at its centre!

Seekers of stone circles may well be disappointed by the offerings of the moors. Although evidence of the Bronze Age is extensive and relatively undisturbed there are no truly dramatic monuments. Stone circles, such as they are, amount to little more than kerbs of small stones such as at Harland Moor and Sleddale and on Danby Rigg a five-foot high slab is the sole survivor of a forty-five-foot circle. There is, however, doubt whether they are all true circles, or simply the retaining kerbs of long dug-away burial mounds, such as the circle called the Bridestones at Cloughton.

In the late Bronze Age, territorial boundaries were emphasized or marked by linear dykes running considerable distances along plateaux and ridges, and perhaps also by shorter cross-dykes over necks of hill spurs, particularly between the dales to the south of Eskdale, though these could be of a later date.

Standing stone, Danby Rigg. The only survivor of a forty-five-foot diameter circle of four.

The extensive Scamridge Dyke system, north of Snainton, and the Cleave Dyke system in the Hambleton Hills comprise complex series of banks and ditches. While it is thought that, together with natural features of the terrain, they delineate territories, some unanswered questions remain. Why, for example, are there several parallel dykes in the Scamridge system beside the car park near the entrance to Troutsdale, when a single dyke would suffice to define a boundary? Perhaps these multiple dykes marked more important or richer territories, but whatever their precise purpose, they are an indication, along with the development of the first hillforts at Boltby and Eston Nab, of the way society was turning in the late Bronze Age. Sadly Boltby Fort, an enclosure with a three-foot-high rampart, was almost totally destroyed by ploughing in 1958.

Other forts, at Roulston Scar, discovered in 1969 and now destroyed, at Live Moor, discovered in 1979 and yet to be excavated and at Horn Nab overlooking Farndale, cannot be accurately dated and could originate either in the Bronze or Iron Age.

The evolution of greater territorial competition and wealthier strata in society are seen in the artefacts of the age too. In addition to functional domestic and agricultural tools, they now included military equipment and ornamental goods.

Most Bronze Age settlements probably lay in the valleys, where, like so much evidence of the past, they have been destroyed by subsequent ploughing, or covered by soil washed down from the hills. Some sites have, however, survived in dale heads and over one whole district of the western moors. For these we can thank the geology. In almost all the major valleys stream erosion cut down through the sandstones and into the Lias, with a resultant improvement in the agricultural potential of the soils. Around Hawnby and Snilesworth it has not cut so deep. This renders the soil far less suitable for arable cultivation and consequently less likely to be disturbed by ploughing.

Originally the soils of the hills were much better than they are today, even though their quality had begun to suffer a little in Mesolithic and Neolithic times. Where woodland was cleared from the tops for arable and pastoral farming soils were thin, vulnerable to erosion and at risk from leaching of their nutrients by the weather. In some locations, after perhaps just a few crops their goodness was depleted and the farmers forced to move on. In others the soil washed away, exposing stony ground. The stones were heaped-up into cairns, but as erosion continued the soils became thinner and poorer. To keep fields clear, cairns grew bigger and more numerous, varying from a few on Live Moor to many hundreds at Iron Howe on Snilesworth Moor, Crown End and Danby Rigg. Usually the cairns are associated with tumbled remains of field walls, constructed to protect crops from free-ranging animals. About seventy of these so called 'cairn-fields' are known in the North York Moors.

Eventually upland farming on the sandstone areas collapsed, with considerable effects on a population ill organized to cope. The degeneration of the soils which began on a small scale in Mesolithic times was virtually complete. Heath spread rapidly, from which the historic forest never recovered.

One cannot help but feel there is a salutary lesson somewhere in the crash of Bronze Age farming for our modern society, which punishes the soil in lowland Britain, though I doubt whether we'll take much notice. Soil erosion on this scale is not just a thing of the past. It is a very real feature in present-day Africa and like the dust bowls of America in the early twentieth century it could also happen again here.

During the Iron Age, from about 650 BC, the population continued to rise in the Tabular Hills, valleys and surrounding countryside. The distribution of Iron Age beehive querns – hand mills for making flour – indicate that the pattern of arable farming may well have been similar to today. Most querns were made from local sandstone, though a small proportion are Millstone Grit from the Pennines. Some can even be linked directly with the quern 'factories' at Goathland, Spaunton Moor and Bransdale, where they were made.

Some farms persisted on the higher ground. A rather impoverished Iron Age farm lies on Percy Rigg and a few miles away on Great Ayton Moor another, built in open grassland about 400 BC, comprised an oval, paved hut with enclosures for crops and stock.

On Levisham Moor, iron was worked in a bloomery in one of a number of huts. When it was discovered the clay dome and bowl-shaped furnace were still intact. A similar furnace operated in the settlement at Roxby, alongside the road towards Scaling, and iron slag in the prehistoric enclosure at Crown End, Castleton, suggests it was worked there too.

Hawnby. Poorer soils, leading to less intensive agriculture, have meant that more archaeological remains have survived in the valleys of this district than valleys elsewhere in the moors.

Whereas the round barrow belonged predominantly to the Bronze Age, the square barrow, which is confined to the eastern part of Yorkshire, was the Iron Age memorial of the district. However, erosion frequently clipped-off the corners, turning them visually into round barrows. A prominent square barrow stands at the top of Carlton Bank, but in the moors most are found on the Tabular Hills where two excavated at Cawthorn Camps and Pexton Moor revealed metal wheel hoops and fragments of wood and harness – remains of 'Chariot Burials', a Continental ritual. Other square barrows have been excavated in the Yorkshire Wolds.

In AD 70 when the Romans arrived in North Yorkshire, the moors probably looked much as they do today, though perhaps with more scrubby birch woodland. On the native British farms, the Iron Age life-style hung on, but by the second and third centuries many of the marginal farms occupied at the beginning of Roman times, such as Percy Rigg, Great Ayton Moor and Levisham Moor, had fallen into disuse, perhaps through continuing decline of soil fertility.

Prior to attacking the native Brigantians in Durham and Northumberland to take the north of England, the Romans established garrisons at York and Malton. Despite the proximity of these centres, only a handful of major Roman sites lie in the park – forts at Lease Rigg and Cawthorn Camps and the foundations of one of the best preserved sections of Roman road, Wade's Causeway, visible where it crosses Wheeldale Moor. This Roman road probably left the Malton to Hovingham road near

Wade's Causeway, Wheeldale Moor. The stones we see today are the foundations, not the surface, of this Roman road.

Amotherby on the north side of the Howardian Hills, heading across the Vale of Pickering to Cawthorn, then on to Lease Rigg, beyond which there is no trace. However it may have continued to an as yet undiscovered destination north of the Esk Valley.

Local legend tells a different story of its origin. Wade, the giant, who it is said sculptured the Hole of Horcum, also reputedly made 'Wade's Causeway' to take cattle to market. While he worked on the road, his wife, Belle, concerned herself with the construction of Mulgrave Castle. They only had one hammer to carry out the work and threw it back and forwards eighteen miles between them. However delightful they may be, 'tall' stories are not needed to fire our imagination about the causeway. The wide, stone road thrusting across the open, lonely moorland is ample in itself to set the mind wondering.

Lease Rigg Fort, a timber-framed structure, with headquarters, commander's home, granary, barracks and stables, was erected some time between AD 80 and 90. Cawthorn Camps, roughly halfway between Lease Rigg and Malton, probably functioned in part as an auxiliary fort, though it is likely that some of the unique square compounds were constructed as part of a field training exercise.

Coastal defences erected in southern England to guard against Saxon raiders were eventually also built between the Tees and Filey at the end of the fourth century. Fortified signalling towers placed at four prominent locations – Scarborough, Ravenscar, Huntcliffe and Goldsborough – relayed messages of intruders to the Roman fleet and/or inland garrisons. At Scarborough the foundations can still be seen on the cliff edge near the castle; Ravenscar has completely gone, perhaps under the Raven Hall Hotel, most of Huntcliffe has fallen into the sea and at Goldsborough, a quarter of a mile inland, the site is now little more than a few humps in a field.

In the early fifth century the signal stations met violent ends, when the sites were sacked, buildings burnt and occupants killed. While this probably happened before AD 410 when the Romans withdrew from Britain, it could have conceivably occurred in the Saxon raids which continued after they had gone. However, no general violent invasion followed in the Romans' footsteps. After their departure the local British population carried on without the central organization of their old overlords and at a lesser or greater rate the Roman way of life faded away.

# 5 Angles, Saxons and Vikings

Continued incursions along the coast and into the
Humber estuary preceded Anglian settlements in
Holderness, the Yorkshire Wolds and the Lower
Trent and Ouse Valleys. We owe the name England
to the Angles and collectively these settlers, along
with other Germanic tribes – the Saxons and Jutes –
later became known as the Anglo-Saxons, a term
apparently first coined by early Continental writers
to differentiate between the Saxons in England and
those elsewhere in mainland Europe.

At first, movement northwards towards the moors
was very slow. Only settlements at Saltburn and
Robin Hood's Bay had developed from the sea by
AD 500. Judging by the size of the pagan cemetery
at the latter, a substantial clifftop community or
village had been established there.

In time Angles moved in greater numbers from
the Wolds into the southern districts of the moors
and inland from the coast. Although there is some
dispute about the origin of place-names, it is
possible that their settlements were given names
ending in '-ing', for example Pickering; '-ham', for
example Wykeham; and '-ingham', for example
Lastingham. They also used '-leah', a clearing in
woodland, and '-tun', an enclosed farmstead, the old
versions of '-ley', for example Helmsley and '-ton',
for example Hutton. A large proportion of these
place-name endings were then prefixed with the
name of the person or group of people who founded
the original farmstead, or a significant feature in the
settlement's surroundings.

What happened to the existing population? Some
may have moved westwards in the face of the
invaders, though others possibly stayed put, with a
change of rulers, but probably little alteration to
their way of life. It seems that Britons may well have
lived alongside Angles in the North York Moors,
though whether they integrated or not is uncertain.
Unfortunately the surviving British place-names are
too few to shed much light on the relationship
between the British and Anglian communities.

By the end of the sixth century the moors were
embraced within the Northumbrian kingdom of

Lilla Cross takes its name from Lilla, a minister to King Edwin, who was buried in the barrow on which the cross stands. In the past crosses were often used as waymarks in rough, featureless or treacherous countryside.

Deira. Christianity came to this pagan society in 627 when Edwin, King of Northumbria, was converted and baptized along with a number of his subjects by Paulinus, a Roman missionary, brought to the north by Edwin's wife, Princess Aethelburgh of Kent.

One year earlier Edwin had survived an assassination attempt at his palace near the River Derwent, either at Malton or Buttercrambe. He only escaped certain death when Lilla, one of his chief ministers, flung himself between the king and the assailant's poisoned dagger.

Lilla was given an elaborate burial in an existing Bronze Age round barrow on Fylingdales Moor, ever since known as Lilla Howe. Some time later a cross was placed on his grave. Lilla Cross, one of the oldest Christian monuments in northern England, is almost certainly the most ancient cross in the North York Moors.

When Fylingdales Moor became a military training ground in 1952, Lilla Cross was moved to a safer place alongside the Whitby to Pickering road. But a decade later a local initiative returned it to the original site, now curiously contrasted by Fylingdales Early Warning Station, its nearest neighbour, on the open moor.

About the same time as Lilla's burial another

funeral took place on a hill above Hawnby, where an important young woman, clad in a gold-clasped girdle, with gold and silver pins in her hair, a bronze bowl placed at her head and surrounded with other ornaments, was interred in a barrow. From these two burials it is clear there was at least some movement up into the dales and on to the moors.

Following the conversion to Christianity two monastic houses were founded, one at Lastingham and the other at Streanashalch (now Whitby).

The guide-book for St Mary's Church, Lastingham, built on the site of the original monastery, boldly announces:

'Brothers we are treading where the Saints have trod.'

This is no idle statement.

The earliest history of Lastingham comes from the Venerable Bede's *History of the English Church and People*, completed at Jarrow monastery in 731. Bede explained that when Cedd was Bishop of the East Saxons he often visited his native Northumbria to preach. In 654 Ethelwald, who ruled the province of Deira at that time, gave Cedd some land on which to found a monastery, where he, Ethelwald, might go to pray and also be buried. Cedd chose the site 'among some high and remote hills which seemed more suitable for the dens of robbers and haunts of wild beasts than for human habitation'.

The purpose of this was apparently to fulfil a prophecy of Isiah:

'In the haunts where dragons once dwelt shall be pasture, with reeds and rushes'

Cedd wished: 'the fruits of good works to spring up where formerly lived only wild beasts, or even men who lived like the beasts'.

Were Cedd, or Bede, or both exaggerating about the depth of the wilderness? Lastingham lies at the foot of the Tabular Hills on the edge of the moors, where a prosperous farming economy once thrived in the Bronze and Iron Ages and during Roman times. If Bede's account is accurate it gives a clear image of the degree to which the local community had degenerated by the seventh century.

In 1846, D H Haigh claimed that St Gregory's Minster in Kirkdale, not Lastingham, was the true site of Cedd's monastery. He maintained that a coffin lid with runic inscriptions belonged to King Ethelwald and another to St Cedd. But there has been little support for this theory.

Three years after the foundation of Lastingham, in 657, King Oswy of Northumbria gave to Hilda, his niece, land on an exposed clifftop where she founded a double monastery for monks and nuns. Streanashalch, her monastery, would become one of the great religious centres of north-east England with among its members Caedmon, the earliest English Christian poet.

During the mid-seventh century considerable friction existed between the Celtic Church, which had largely converted the north, and the Roman Church, which had worked from the south. Disagreements about the date of Easter finally brought matters to a head and in 664 the Synod of Whitby was summoned to settle the issue once and for all.

St Hilda, along with St Coleman of Lindisfarne, supported the Celtic system. Opposing them was St Wilfred of Ripon. In conclusion, Oswy accepted the Roman view and thus the dating of Easter was set for us all on the windswept clifftops of Whitby nearly 1,400 years ago. This decision also signalled the retreat of the Celtic Church. Overlooking the coast from the top of Blue Bank you can readily appreciate what a wild and exposed place it must have been.

King Edwin was slain at Hatfield Chase near Doncaster in 633. Later his body was exhumed and brought to Whitby for burial. However, his head was taken to York and buried in the church – a forerunner of York Minster – which he had founded there.

In 680 a 'daughter house' was settled at Hackness from the monastery at Whitby. No recorded history of the area then exists until 867 when all three monasteries and other smaller churches which may have developed under their influence were sacked by the Vikings.

There were two waves of Scandinavian invasion – by Danes in the ninth century and Norwegians, who, had previously settled in Ireland, in the tenth. It is a tradition that the Danes Ingwar and Ubba destroyed the monastery at Whitby, though the Danes do not seem to have settled in that district to any great extent.

Soon after their arrival the Vikings adopted Christianity. Having first knocked churches down, they then set about re-establishing new ones, recognizing both old and new sites by the inclusion of 'kir(k)by', from the Old Norse *kirkja* – farmstead by the church – in place-names, such as

Autumn at Danby Lodge, the Moors Centre. Danby was one of the isolated settlements founded by the Viking invaders from Denmark.

Kirkbymoorside, and Cold Kirkby.

Both Danes and Norse commonly used the place-name endings '-*by*' and '-*thorpe*'; -*by*, when coupled with a person's name, denoted a farm or hamlet, in names such as Aislaby, Brawby and Normanby to the south of the park; Boltby, Thirkleby, Ingleby and Easby to the west; and more isolated settlements inland from Whitby at Danby and Ugglebarnby – the farm of the man nicknamed 'Owl-beard'; -*thorpe* described a hamlet from an existing village, thus Fylingthorpe is an offshoot of Fyling near Robin Hood's Bay. However, many of the communities with Viking names probably result from the renaming of existing settlements.

Other than place-names the mix of cultures from the ninth, tenth and eleventh centuries – Anglo-Danish, Anglo-Norse, and a drop of Irish for good measure – can also be found in the remnants of ancient Christian monuments.

Pre-Viking Anglian crosses are rare in the park. Lilla is the best example. Its good condition and imposing location on Fylingdales Moor make it superficially the most attractive. However, the sections of an Anglian cross shaft, with Runic and Latin inscriptions, in Hackness church are intrinsically more revealing of its origins.

Part of the inscription on it reads:

> 'O Aethelburga . . . may thy houses ever be mindful of thee, most loving mother . . . Abbess Aethelburga pray ye for us.'

Fragments of Anglian churchyard crosses are often found in the stone walls of Saxon churches.

Distinct carved designs belong to each ensuing culture. At the end of the seventh century Anglian crosses depicted interlaced panels with figures, leaves, birds and animals mixed with scrolls. On Anglo-Danish crosses, dragons sometimes replaced the animals and at Ellerburn carvings on the cross fragments where the dragon becomes entangled within its own tongue and tail display the tenth-century Norse influence. Another Norse cross shaft stands in Hawsker churchyard near Whitby. Additional Irish-Norse characteristics can be traced in a range of fragments at Lastingham, St Gregory's, Kirkbymoorside, Helmsley, Ellerburn and Levisham.

Churches built after the Viking invasions were initially wooden, but in the eleventh century widespread rebuilding with stone took place. Described today as 'Saxon', these structures sometimes incorporated pieces of old stone crosses which once stood in their churchyards.

Ellerburn church.

The hog-back tombstone, representing a long, low house is another form of early religious stone carving. A more elaborate version, 'The Bear Hog-backs' to be seen at Osmotherley and Lastingham, shows a bear stretched across the roof, clasping the 'gables' at either end.

Perhaps one of the most important pieces of stone carving was discovered tucked under a porch and above a doorway in 1771 at St Gregory's Minster, Kirkdale. During building work an elaborately inscribed Saxon sundial – the most complete of its kind in the world – was uncovered below a layer of plaster. The inscription tells us precisely about its origin:

> 'Orm, Gamel's son bought St Gregory's minster when it was all ruined and fallen down, and he caused it to be built new from the ground in the days of Edward and in the days of Tosti the earl. This is the day's sun marker at each hour. Haworth made me and Brand, priests.'

The reference to Tostig, brother of King Harold, who was Earl of Northumberland in 1055 and banished in 1065, allows a close dating of the rebuilding of St Gregory's Minster. One might reasonably wonder what earthly use a sundial under a porch would be. Absolutely none, but the porch was not there when the sundial was put in position.

# 6 **Monasteries**

It is 1066, and all change. Harold of Wessex – King Harold – has defeated Harald Hardrada, King of Norway, at the Battle of Stamford Bridge near York.

But the euphoria of success was short lived. Having marched his forces south, Harold was subsequently killed and his army defeated by William of Normandy at the Battle of Hastings.

Initially William hoped to govern with the support of the established English aristocracy. But following rebellions by powerful earls he reviewed his policies, ruthlessly put down the opposition in a Blitzkreig known as the 'Harrying of the North', adopted an iron rule, built castles, dispossessed the holders of thousands of small estates, redrew their boundaries into just 200 large feudal holdings and installed Norman barons.

Having established his authority, William then set about a survey of the entire country. Domesday Book of 1086 records sixty-nine separate places in the North York Moors. It is in this survey that the first detailed information of the Anglo-Saxon and Viking place-names are recorded.

Immediately after the Conquest a resurgence of monasticism swept across the country. Monks, particularly the Cistercians, seeking remote places such as the North Yorks Moors to escape from the wickedness of the world, found landowners with huge tracts of poor land willing and able to dedicate large areas to the monks in which they could settle and construct their houses.

When the major monasteries were founded in the eleventh and twelfth centuries the area to which the monks came was mostly an uncultivated wilderness of natural growth, wild scrubby moorland and marsh. The wasted and soulful character of the countryside resulted largely from the effects of William's 'Harrying of the North'. One writer of the time described such a site as a 'place of horror and waste solitude'.

At first, obviously, there were no permanent monastic buildings. The only shelter was probably mud or wooden huts – little protection against the cold harsh winter weather of these parts. Grazing

Saxon sundial, St Gregory's Minster, Kirkdale.

for stock had to be established and crops grown. But before the land could be farmed the ground had to be cleared. Preparations also had to be made for the construction of permanent buildings. A visitor to this area in the eleventh century would have found a very wild and remote place, where living was far from easy.

After the Conquest, Benedictines were the first order to build a major monastery in the moors. At Whitby in 1074, they founded their house close by the ruins of St Hilda's seventh-century Celtic monastery. In the years to come, the Benedictines settled a further five sites in the region. Other religious orders followed – Augustinian Canons, Cistercians, Crutched Friars, Grandimontines, Knights Templars, Knights Hospitalers and Carthusians.

Of all the orders to settle here the Cistercians had the greatest impact. Their rule demanded a life of utmost simplicity, self-sufficiency and divorce from the secular world with a consequent and considerable commitment to agriculture for survival.

The first Cistercian house in the area was founded in 1131 at Rievaulx, near Helmsley, on land

Rievaulx Abbey in Ryedale, a truly romantic rural scene. Unfortunately the magnificent elm tree had now fallen to the ravages of Dutch elm disease.

dedicated to the monks by Walter L'Espec of
Helmsley.

On the banks of the River Rye the monks set about
the task of developing their buildings: due to the
narrowness of the site the abbey was orientated
north–south instead of the customary east–west.
However, it became evident that self-sufficiency and
adherence to the strict Cistercian rule, which
required considerable attention to spiritual matters,
did not go well together: there were simply not
enough hours in the day. To overcome this general
problem a new class of monk – the lay brother – was
created. Lay brothers were not required to devote
so much time to the spiritual side of monastic life.
This left them free to spend more hours working.

There is a traditional view that monks were great
teachers within the community. While some, such as
the Benedictines, were indeed teaching orders,
there is nothing to show that the Cistercians did
anything in particular for the education of the local
community. Nor even do they appear to have
improved the learning of their own lay brothers,
whose level of education often remained the same
as the day they entered the monastery. However,
the Cistercians did come to provide considerable
indirect employment for the local inhabitants.

Monks chose their sites with great care. There
had to be an adequate supply of fresh water, usually
from springs, for drinking, and a sufficient flow to
carry away sewage.

Construction of an abbey was a considerable task
and additions or alterations were often made at a
later date. At Rievaulx, work started shortly after the
monks' arrival. Although much of the construction
took place in the last sixty years of the twelfth
century, major building still continued during the
thirteenth and other work as late as the fifteenth
century.

With the establishment and success of the abbeys,
new lands, often in considerable numbers, were
granted to them. The Cistercians were highly
successful farmers, but it is their abilities with sheep
farming and wool production in particular for which
they are most remembered. Certainly they were
responsible for the early development of large-
scale moorland grazing and as new lands were
granted to the monasteries the granges (farms)
stretched far from the abbey precincts. There are
estimated to have been at least 12,000 sheep in
Rievaulx's flock, and between 50,000 and 60,000 in
the area as a whole at the end of the thirteenth

century. Rievaulx controlled granges up to twenty miles away– too far to travel daily for working. A number of lay brothers, under a prior, were therefore assigned to the granges, only journeying back to the abbey for mass on perhaps three occasions each year. It is ironic that the poor lands given away by the landowners should be the most appropriate for exploitation to satisfy the considerable demand for wool in medieval times.

Although best known as sheep farmers, Cistercians were by no means restricted in their pursuits; crop-production, milling, beekeeping and charcoal and much of the early iron-working, as well as general skills in land and forest management, came within the compass of their activities. Both lay and monastic iron industries worked in the dales. Byland Abbey owned furnaces in Rosedale; Rievaulx owned some in Bilsdale; and the Augustinian priory at Guisborough had furnaces in Glaisdale.

Other monasteries controlled granges too. Where monks had to cross large tracts of open land, monks' trods developed. Some of them were paved and survive today. In the northern parts of the moor it is probable that monks from Guisborough used them to walk to their granges in the Esk Valley. Another can be traced from Grosmont, where there was a priory, to Whitby Abbey. Not all paved ways are monks' trods, others are pannier-ways. But their purposes were the same: to enable easier progress for man and pack animals across the boggy moors in all weather conditions.

All told there were twenty-five sites of medieval religious houses established in the region between the Norman Conquest and Henry VIII's Dissolution of the monasteries. However, of these sites only fourteen are known to have still been active at the end. Of the others some simply failed or died out, and several were vacated for new locations.

The monks who eventually ended up at Byland Abbey near Coxwold arrived by a circuitous route. Having left Furness in Lancashire they settled initially at Hood Grange below Sutton Bank in 1138, then moved to a new site north of Rievaulx in 1143 where they founded the village of Old Byland which still retains its medieval layout today. Here, so the legend goes, the bells of Rievaulx got on the nerves of the monks at Old Byland and the bells of Old Byland got on the nerves of the monks at Rievaulx. Since they had come for peace and quiet, bells ringing all the time could not be tolerated, so

A monks' trod above Commondale near the Castleton to Lockwood Beck road.

someone had to go. It was the Old Byland group which moved again. This time to Stocking and finally, after a further thirty years, in 1177 to the site of Byland Abbey. The true reasons for the move are probably much more twentieth-century sounding than the explanation of ringing bells. The Byland group had moved in much too close to Rievaulx's territory and furthermore sewage from the newcomers' establishment would have flowed downstream past the latter's land.

Carthusians were the last order to settle in the moors. In 1398 they established Mount Grace Priory, or, to give it its full title, 'The House of the Assumption of the Most Blessed Virgin and St Nicholas of Mount Grace at Ingleby', near Osmotherley. Today its ruins remain the best preserved evidence of Carthusian monasticism in Britain.

Where Cistercians required separation from the world, Carthusians took it one stage further and demanded a life of utter solitude. Each monk lived in his own cell, with two rooms and a small walled garden. Hermit-like seclusion even extended to a right-angled bend in the hole in the wall through which the monk received his food. This prevented him from seeing the person who had brought it. Life in individual cells obviated the need for a large church, which was therefore small by comparison with those of other orders.

In the late twelfth century there are said to have been 140 monks and 500 lay brothers at Rievaulx. But by the mid-fourteenth century the numbers of many of the houses were drastically reduced by the Black Death. Monasticism was on the wane, in some cases only a handful of monks occupying once crowded abbeys. In many places the observance of the principles of the abbey had become very lax. Many monasteries were now large and powerful landowners, with all the pressures of administration of land and tenants, and abbots had begun to lead more worldly lives, living in a separate house, eating well, and indulging in sports such as hunting and hawking.

When Henry VIII came to the throne there were almost 900 monastic communities in the country. Notwithstanding Henry's jealousy of the abbeys' wealth and his split with Rome over the issue of divorce, for many years there had been a feeling that the smaller monastic houses could be closed to the benefit of all concerned.

In 1536 the Act for the Suppression of the Lesser Monasteries was therefore seen initially as a practical reform. The smaller houses at Arden, Baysdale, Grosmont, Keldholme and Rosedale were all dissolved under this Act. Their properties were in effect nationalized and compensation paid by way of pensions to the senior monks. The remaining monks or nuns were allowed to transfer to a larger monastery, or to give up their vows.

By the summer of 1536 most of the smaller houses had been dissolved, but the rushed manner in which the suppression was carried out, added to many other fears and discontentment, brought strong objections. In 1536 a northern rebellion, 'The Pilgrimage of Grace', was ruthlessly put down by the King. Five leading abbots were executed for treason and their abbeys and lands confiscated by the Crown. The writing was clearly on the wall. Some leading abbots began voluntarily to surrender, the conditions at first being the same as for the smaller abbeys. By 1537, however, this offer was dropped, and all the monks and nuns were pensioned off.

Rievaulx surrendered in 1538; Byland, Mount Grace and Whitby the following year; and Guisborough Priory early in 1540. By March 1540 there were no monastic religious houses in England and Wales.

Rievaulx Terraces and Temples, near Helmsley, with magnificent views over the abbey.

With the surrender bells were removed, abbey roofs dismantled and timbers burned to melt the lead. This was then shipped away and turned into lead shot.

Stripped of their roofs the buildings soon deteriorated. Masonry was removed to build or repair farm buildings and walls. Over the centuries the abbeys degenerated in a progressive state of ruin, clad in creepers and wild plants. Today many have gone for ever or, like Rosedale, can only be located by a few stones. However, four major sites have passed into the hands of English Heritage to be preserved – Byland, near Coxwold, Rievaulx, near Helmsley, Whitby Abbey and Guisborough Priory. Mount Grace Priory, which is owned by the National Trust, is also managed by English Heritage.

# 7 Churches, crosses and castles

A ruin often conveys much greater feeling of antiquity than a complete building, even though it may be of lesser age. The tumbled structures of the major monastic houses distract us from the earlier origins of many local churches, which have been maintained, repaired, altered or extended since Saxon times. During the last 1,000 years, some have become composite expressions of the masons' and carpenters' handiwork over the centuries.

Typically the oldest churches show numerous phases of construction. At Hackness a late Saxon chancel forms the earliest work. The south arcade is largely Norman, while the north arcade and tower are Early English. Outside, the clerestory and spire, and inside, the chancel stalls and font cover are fifteenth century; the vestry, pulpit and candlesticks date from the seventeenth century and the sections of Anglo-Saxon cross shaft from the seventh-century Celtic nunnery, link back almost to the very origins of organized Christianity in the area.

Similar mixtures of architecture and fittings from different periods are widespread throughout the park, though most of the buildings in which they are found have been subject to restoration, or even rebuilding particularly by late Georgians and Victorians.

Occasionally almost the entire church belongs to one period. St Mary's at Scawton is virtually all Norman and much Norman work exists at Over Silton, St Felix's at Felixkirk, St Hilda's at Ellerburn, and in the interior of St Andrew's at Ingleby Greenhowe, where later masons had a field day sculpting curious capitals on the Norman columns.

Frequently Norman fonts were retained in the new buildings, or brought from other churches. St Hilda's at Sneaton has a reworked example; St Stephen's at Robin Hood's Bay employs one from the Old St Stephen's which fell into disuse in the 1870s; St Aidan's at Gillamoor is possibly Norman, Nether Silton's is an enormous example, and St Mary's at Goathland, built in 1896, has the font from the Egton Church, demolished in 1878.

The part Norman, part Early English, Holy Cross

Coxwold church has a fine octangular tower and interesting stained glass.

at Whorlton has an eerie atmosphere. Approached through a dense grove of yews, the three-quarter ruined church, hemmed in tightly by trees, and overlooked at a distance by the ruined Whorlton Castle, is isolated near the site of its abandoned medieval village.

In the Decorated chancel, viewed through a sort of 'cat flap' halfway up the locked door, a canopied tomb recess houses an early fourteenth-century oak effigy of Nicholas de Meynell looking uncannily as though he's just settled down for an afternoon nap.

In contrast to Whorlton, Danby church, in Danby Dale, is isolated from its community in Eskdale, though still in full use. Canon Atkinson, its most renowned incumbent, was until recent times one of the few people to write about the region. His much sought-after book, *Forty Years In A Moorland Parish*, is a rare insight into the everyday life of the moors in the past.

Every churchyard, memorial or church record preserves a part of the history of its community and district. St Nicholas, Roxby, has an unusual early seventeenth-century black slab monument, supported by white marble urns; St Mary's, Goathland, an altar stone, said to be from the twelfth-century hermitage founded thereabouts and St Anne's Roman Catholic church at Goathland holds the chalice used by Father Nicholas Postgate, who was hanged in 1679. A list of potentially fascinating details would be almost endless. However, on occasions a church has exceptional characteristics which set it apart from the rest. Around the park there are four, each of which has a special place in

St Gregory's Minster, Kirkdale.

the story of churches in Britain. Although three of them are just outside the boundary it would be an omission not to include them here.

St Gregory's Minster, tucked among trees near Hodge Beck in Kirkdale has already been mentioned for its unique Saxon sundial. A narrow arched Saxon doorway now leads into the Victorian tower, and around the walls stone benches provided seating for the old and infirm in the days before pews were introduced. Such arrangements gave rise to the expression 'let the weakest go to the wall'.

Where the sundial is St Gregory's 'trademark' so a unique Norman crypt is that of St Mary's at Lastingham. Built by Stephen Prior from Whitby Abbey in 1078 as a shrine to Sts Cedd and Chad on the site of the seventh-century monastery, it remains virtually unaltered structurally since the day it was finished.

Stephen had planned a full blown abbey on the site, but with only part of the main aisle completed he abandoned the project and moved on to York where he established St Mary's Abbey. The original pillars were subsequently incorporated into the walls of the parish church which followed.

The crypt is reached from the centre of the

church. Passing through the doorway at the foot of
the stairs is a step back through time. When the
electric lights are out it takes several seconds to
adjust to the sudden dark, damp, stillness. As your
eyes become accustomed to the change, soft light
shafting through a narrow slit window falls across a
beautifully simple altar, perhaps the very one the
monks prayed at in their remote monastery long

The unique Norman crypt
of St Mary's church,
Lastingham.

ago. The peace and seclusion tugs you across the
centuries, and if the solitary church bell should ring
high above it will heighten an experience you are
unlikely to forget.

Other than the crypt there are traces of Norman
work in the church, though most is thirteenth
century, the tower fifteenth and the stunning vaulted
stone ceilings a relatively recent (1879) though
admirable addition.

If simplicity is Lastingham's prime quality, then it
is complexity which gives St Mary's at Whitby its
fascination. This squat structure perched on the
clifftop above Whitby is deceptively spacious. With
seating for 1,500, its internal layout is a maze of
galleries and pews. More than anywhere else
St Mary's displays directly an assemblage of the
practical alterations and additions over numerous
generations. An especially intriguing feature is the
roof which, having been replaced by ships'
carpenters, bears more than a passing resemblance
to an old wooden ship's deck. The line of the
previous roof apex can still be traced on the side of
the tower.

In the clifftop churchyard at the top of the 199
steps from the Old Town the blackened,

weatherbeaten gravestones create aesthetically
pleasing shapes and a wonderland for the
photographer. Their fading inscriptions, coursed
through by wind-borne spray and rain, make a
thought-provoking catalogue of life and death by
the sea.

The first-time visitor will be equally surprised on
entering Pickering parish church. Along the upper
wall some of the most complete medieval wall
paintings in the country tell their haunting religious
stories.

Discovered accidentally in 1851, finally
uncovered in 1878, and cleaned in 1937, they depict
various characters and scenes – St George and the
Dragon; St Christopher, Patron Saint of Travellers;
the gruesome martyrdom of St John the Baptist; God
the Father, Son and Holy Ghost are there too, while
above them the Heavenly Host look on. Not for the
squeamish are the martydoms of St Thomas and
St Edmund, who is shot full of arrows, nor the story
of Catherine of Alexandria, to whom the dubious
honour of responsibility for the 'Catherine Wheel' is
attributed – she was tied to a wheel and spun along.

Medieval wall paintings,
St Peter's and St Paul's,
Pickering.

A number of interesting memorials are placed in
the church. One commemorates two Pickering
surveyors named King who helped plan the city of
Washington in the United States. Another in the
north aisle remembers William Marshall, the
agricultural economist who lived nearby in the
house now occupied by the Beck Isle Museum of
Rural Life.

Since the earliest times, the sign of the cross has
been a symbol of Christianity. Used to remind
people about Christ, stone and wooden crosses
have been erected for a variety of reasons. They
marked meeting places, entries to towns, markets,
boundaries and in open featureless countryside the
junction of roads or treacherous and boggy places.
They were also used to commemorate notable
events, murders or sudden and violent deaths.

The earliest crosses were used as preaching
places by Celtic missionaries, though almost all
those surviving in their original locations here are
medieval or later and were most probably
waymarkers. Their relative abundance in the
region led to Ralph Cross being aptly chosen as the
emblem for the North York Moors National Park.
Critics believe a natural feature or animal should
have been used. But the moors, both past and
present, are also very much about people and there
can be no disagreement that the monks of the great

Mauley Cross near Snape.

religious houses, in whose times many of the crosses may well have originated, had a profound influence on the way the park looks today.

Only a handful of the twenty or thirty named crosses or cross sites are graced by a traditionally shaped monument. Most are no more than a base, stump or shaft and of others there is now nothing to see at all. The notable traditional crosses are: 'Young' Ralph, an eighteenth-century replacement for an earlier cross mentioned as a boundary marker of Pickering Lythe in early charters, above Rosedale Head; 'Old' Ralph, a few hundred yards west; ancient Lilla on Fylingdales Moor; Ainehowe, which probably replaced Ana whose fragments are at Lastingham crypt, south of Rosedale Chimney Bank; and Mauley, named after the de Mauleys of Mulgrave Castle, which is now engulfed by a forestry plantation near Snape.

'Old' and 'Young' Ralph and Fat Betty, along with the Margery stone, grouped above Rosedale Head, are probably subjects of more folk tales than all the others put together.

A popular explanation for their names involves a complex escapade in the fog several hundred years ago. 'Old' Ralph was a Rosedale man, so it is said, engaged to accompany the prioresses of Rosedale and Baysdale Abbeys on a walkabout on the moors to resolve a boundary dispute between the two houses. In a dense fog the two women became separated and lost. But 'Old' Ralph found Sister Betty where a cross now bears her name, and Sister Margery by the upright 'Margery' stone half a mile away. Ralph then reunited the two at the site of his own cross.

A wedding is to be confidently expected when 'Young' Ralph and Fat Betty meet, and gloom and foreboding surrounds the time should three kings ever get together there – for then the world will end. A more straightforward story tells that Ralph was simply a Danby man who died in a blizzard.

There are also tales that Fat Betty was a Castleton woman lost overboard from her husband's horse and cart on a dark and foggy night. She'd been travelling in the back and when the farmer arrived at Castleton there was no sign of her. Retracing his route across the moors all he could find was a large squat stone.

Alternatively called White Cross, for the coat of whitewash she regularly receives, Betty's head is a small, ancient wheelhead cross attached to a later base. She stands at the junction of Danby, Westerdale and Rosedale parishes where the old track from Castleton meets the road from Rosedale to Westerdale.

The immediate area of Ralph Cross also commands a place in local weather lore. Some believe if the tops here are covered with snow three times before Christmas then a good winter will follow.

For a fixed object 'Young' Ralph has had a fairly active career over the last twenty-five years. In the early 1960s a man, climbing the cross to see if any coins had been left in the niche in the top – an old tradition to aid needy travellers who might follow you – knocked Ralph over snapping it into three pieces. With repairs effected and the pieces joined by metal splints the cross was replaced, only shortly afterwards to be blown to a jaunty angle by a gale. Once more it was reset. Twenty years later in 1985 worse was to come. Some philistines, using a chain and a vehicle, pulled the cross over, causing irreparable damage. It is difficult to comprehend the purpose of such an insane act – pointless is too weak a word – but in the months Ralph was absent as new parts were sculpted, to those who know and love the moors, an important focus was missing. It could be comparable to the Statue of Liberty without her torch, the Old Bailey without 'Justice' or York Minster with no tower. Overstating the case? Perhaps. But it wasn't the same up there. Ralph Cross, in its remote location, encapsulates something special about the very spirit of the moors.

Lines of crosses can be traced running south from Whitby towards Pickering and west towards Guisborough. Some at least are markers of old road junctions and the names of others, now gone, are preserved on ancient maps and in records.

Along the route probably used by the monks of Whitby to travel to Pickering an ancient churchyard cross stands at Abbey Plain. Nothing now remains of High Normanby, recorded on Knox's 1821 map of Scarborough. Postgate, possibly named after Father Nicholas Postgate, marks the junction of Robin Hood's Bay road; it is followed by John, Anne, Lilla which is recorded in early charters as a boundary of Whitby Strand, and finally Malo, which stood on Whinny Neb in the Tabular Hills.

Details of a cross erected near Whinny Neb – 'neb', 'nab' or 'noddle' are local words for the promontories of the Tabular Hills – are mentioned in the records of the Duchy of Lancaster in connection with an alleged violation of the laws governing the royal deer forest of Pickering:

'In the years 1619 and 1621 various matters, including charge of trespass and encroachment were submitted for the consideration of the jury, who found ''that above 3 or 4 years before the date of this survey, Sir Richard Egerton Kt hath made divers inclosures, about Blackhow being in the heart of the forest, but by what warrant they know not, and hath set or caused to be set up on whynny neb a new bounderstone, with a cross and directeth to Ellerbeck head over Wormsike, to Lillhow crosse . . .'''

'Young' Ralph Cross stands near the very highest part of the moors.

Working westwards from Whitby, Swarth Howe Cross stands where the old Whitby road crosses the boundary of Whitby Strand, and Stump cross at the junction of the track to Scaling, east of Danby · Beacon. Following the high ground Siss Cross, now replaced by a modern stone, lies two miles westwards; Job, one mile further still at the junction with the Castleton to Moorsholme track, and in another half a mile a different White Cross identifies the crossroads with the main Castleton to Lockwood Beck road. The upper parts of its predecessor are now in Whitby Museum. Percy Cross then stands beside another track across the moors from Baysdale to Guisborough.

Little evidence exists to link named crosses with real people, save for Lilla, Mauley and perhaps Postgate, and the precise purpose for which many were erected is committed to the proverbial mists of time. Raising of monuments at the wayside or in prominent positions is an enduring tradition. The substantial obelisk on Easby Moor in honour of Captain James Cook and the beautifully understated and simply inscribed boulder to Frank Elgee above Rosedale Head remember two significant people of the moors. Memorials in towns and villages record a lasting recognition of gratitude to local people who have been killed in wars. But a small stone marker in Lealholm perhaps comes closest to one of the possible historical reasons for raising crosses on the moors – to mark a tragedy. An inscription on the small stone recalls Major Donald L Schuyler and Lieutenant Thomas D Wheeler who died on the hillside, when their United States Air Force plane came down narrowly missing the village. The men

Captain Cook's Monument, Easby Moor, is one of the landmarks of the North York Moors.

A scene in the Bayeux Tapestry shows a soldier escaping from the look-out tower of a motte and bailey style Norman castle.

had stayed at the controls and the people of Lealholm wished to remember them.

One day, when the weather has worn away the inscription of our monuments, their origins, like those of the lonely crosses of the moor, may well become equally obscure.

Alongside the world of religious building the centuries following the Norman Conquest were the heyday of the castle. These fortified residences, introduced by the Normans, provided protection for their owners during skirmishes, especially with the Scots, but they were also a straightforward and outward show of baronial power.

The earliest motte and bailey castles were stepped, split-level arrangements. A look-out tower was often placed atop a steep mound (the motte) and surrounded by a palisade (strong fence). The residence was usually constructed at the lower level in a large fortified compound (the bailey) where the defensive forces were also garrisoned. None of the original Norman wooden castles has survived in the moors, but a contemporary illustration in the Bayeaux Tapestry gives a simplistic impression of what one looked like. There was however an inherent drawback. Whether by accident or attack, wooden castles were vulnerable to destruction by fire.

Stone provided the only alternative, though at a substantial increase in the cost of construction. Wooden structures at Pickering and Whorlton were replaced by stone keeps in the early twelfth century and extended later with even more elaborate defences. Those at Cropton, Easby, Brompton, Felixkirk and Hood Hill fell into disuse or were destroyed and at Foss, near Lythe, and Castleton, were abandoned for other nearby sites.

Robert de Stuteville's Cropton Castle, overlooking Rosedale, can only be traced by the earthworks of its 150-foot diameter motte and three-acre bailey. Likewise mounds are the main clues to the locations where many of the others once stood. Easby's tree-covered motte is positioned conspicuously above a steep bank, Brompton's to the east of the village and Felixkirk's at a road junction in the centre. Kildale's has been partly cut away by the Middlesbrough to Whitby railway, whereas at Hood Hill the site is so overgrown as to be virtually unrecognizable.

In 1197 Foss Castle, built in 1071 by Nigel Fossard, was abandoned in favour of a new stone structure at Mulgrave, which Robert de Turnham completed in

the early thirteenth century. One hundred years
later this was itself in ruins, although it remained
standing for another three hundred years before
being largely dismantled in 1647. Parts of the towers
and walls still stand on the precipice above
Sandsend Beck.

At Castleton, where the Guisborough road now
skirts the mound, Robert de Brus's castle was
similarly abandoned and dismantled in 1216.
However, over a century elapsed before the lords
of the manor took up residence at Danby, in a
strategic position overlooking Eskdale. The
remains of this palace/fortress of the Latimer and
later the de Neville families include sections of the
massive square towers, walls and the dungeons as
well as the coat of arms of the de Nevilles on the
south wall. The castle is still a working farm and not
open to the public. However, good views of it can be
gained from the roadside and surrounding hills.

The word 'castle' describes a number of different
types of building. It applies to the popular concept
of turreted forts which developed between the
Norman Conquest and the fifteenth century. It also
applies to later fortified manor houses, and even
more recent buildings, such as Sneaton Castle,
which are merely decorative, castellated, country
houses.

Whereas fire exposed the weaknesses of the
Norman wooden castles, increasing fire-power and
improvements in techniques of attack gradually
reduced the effectiveness of stone defences. With
steady development in weaponry the walls could no
longer guarantee security. Apart from this, the
powers of feudal society focused on the large
landowners had begun to diminish as Parliament
took greater control of the country. With
developing trade there were stronger needs to
protect whole towns and communities rather than
simply the homes of the rich and powerful.

Most of the twenty-eight 'castles', or sites, in and
around the North York Moors are on private land.
But Scarborough, Ayton, Helmsley, Pickering and
Whorlton Castles are open to the public and the
ruined Mulgrave Castle is accessible on certain
days, by courtesy of its owner, the Marquis of
Normanby.

Castle Hill, Scarborough, has been a defensive
position since prehistoric and Roman times.
Between 1135 and 1138, during the reign of King
Stephen, William de Gros constructed the oldest
parts of the present building. These were later

Entrance to Helmsley
Castle.

upgraded into a stronger keep and bailey in
1158–68 and the barbican was added in 1343. After
the sieges of the Civil War, the Castle was
converted into a prison where George Fox, founder
of the Quaker movement was held in 1665–6.

Ayton Castle, a fortified manor house, was
completed in about 1400 to replace the original,
built by William de Ayton in 1180. Last occupied at
the end of the seventeenth century, it was partly
pulled down following the death of the then owner,
Edmund Mauleverer. Some stone from the ruins was
subsequently used in the rebuilding of Ayton
Bridge in 1775.

On the western flanks of the moors near Swainby,
Whorlton Castle, the fourteenth-century fortified
home of the Meynell family, commands a fine view
over the entrance to Scugdale. Here a stone tower
and gatehouse replaced the wooden buildings. Its
history can be traced through details in the ruins.
Shields bearing the 'arms' of the Meynell, D'Arcy
and Gray families who lived here between the early
twelfth century and 1342 and a larger shield
carrying the 'arms' of Philip D'Arcy's son-in-law, Sir
James Strangeways, are carved above the gateway.
Slits above and to either side of the entrance were
used for the chains or ropes by which a drawbridge
over the deep moat was operated.

During the Civil War, Oliver Cromwell's troops
destroyed much of the building, by then the home of
Thomas, Lord Bruce: scars from the cannon attack
can still be seen on the stonework. Afterwards a
manor house was erected to the west side by
Robert, Earl of Ailesbury, the son of Lord Bruce. Its
roof line is also still visible on the wall.

Within the park, Helmsley, and just outside the
park, Pickering Castles present the most extensive
ruins for the visitor. Helmsley, although of little
significance in historical times, gives a good
impression of the layout of the tower, domestic
buildings, defensive curtain wall and ditches. Of
particular note are the unusual and innovative
'D'-shaped keep and impressive and progressive
gatehouse towers. The oldest parts date from the
mid-twelfth century but many major sections such as
kitchen, buttery and great hall were added during
the fourteenth and fifteenth centuries.

Pickering has had a more distinguished past.
Although not noted for any part in the cut and thrust
of history, it was nevertheless visited by most of the
kings of England between 1100 and 1400. They used
it as a hunting lodge for the Royal Hunting Forest of

Pickering created about 1106 by King Henry I.

The modern understanding of the word forest as continuous woodland is quite different from its Norman meaning. Then it referred to an area where special laws protected the game and trees. It would have encompassed open ground, marsh and even villages, as well as woodland. Several manors lay within the forest boundaries, which stretched from west of Sinnington to Ralph Cross, Goathland and the coast. But the laws were such that not even the lords of these manors were allowed to hunt their own land unless licensed by the king or his justice.

Forest law not only protected the animals but also their environment as well. Woodland was termed the 'vert', of which there were several categories: 'high vert' – mature trees; 'nether-vert' – shrubs and bushes; and 'special-vert' – which included fruit-bearing trees. Virtually everything growing seems to have been protected in one way or another. There was a sound logic to this. In order to conserve the animals, it was essential firstly to protect where they lived. This obvious and basic principle seems frequently to be lost on our twentieth-century society, which demands the conservation of wildlife, but seems unable to grasp the need for laws which will unequivocally safeguard its home.

The world of the hunting forest gave rise to its own specialized language to describe the animals and their behaviour. Some of the terms are still in common use – a 'slot' refers to a deer footprint and a 'trace' to a line of them. Deer whose antlers are growing are said to be in 'velvet' and 'fraying' identifies where the animals have rubbed their antlers against trees. Interestingly deer fat was known as 'sewet'.

The ordinary population of the townships within the forest had certain rights to take wood. Dry sticks could be gathered, but larger timbers for house building, hedging and fencing, or for making agricultural implements such as ploughs, could only be obtained under supervision. This way the king's forester exercised control over which trees were being removed. Taking of wood was not 'a right' and even collecting sticks was considered to be 'at the King's Will' and an annual payment made that was relative to the size of holding.

There were however some serious flaws in the forest law. Existing trees and shrubbery were protected, but no adequate precautions were taken to ensure new saplings could regenerate from seed.

Over-grazing, along with removal of too much timber, both legally and illegally, reduced the woodland cover. Over-hunting also took its toll. By 1360 no wild boar were left and 200 years later deer were thin on the ground. By royal proclamation a moratorium on hunting was enforced and new laws to fence off areas to exclude both deer and domestic animals were introduced to give saplings a chance to grow. But they were too late. In the 1640s farmers north of Pickering applied to Parliament to be relieved from the outdated forest laws: disemparkment followed.

The loss of woodland had profound effects on the iron-making industry in the dales. In many ways this was its own fault, for the furnaces were rapacious consumers of charcoal.

With the depletion of woodland, the introduction of coal-fired blast furnaces elsewhere and competition from cheaper foreign iron from countries such as Sweden and Russia, the early iron industry of the dales faded. It was an economic fact of life, not helped by the upheaval of the Civil War.

The shortage of charcoal had an impact on domestic users too. They turned their attention to peat, turfs and coal. The peat and turfs were cut from the moor and the coal mined in small, family run, bell-pits. The name originates from the shape of the hollow excavated underground and care had to be taken not to undermine the lip of the pit too much for fear of collapse. Their doughnut-shaped spoil-heaps are evident in many places throughout the moors.

Moor coal was poor quality stuff and had to be mixed with peat and charcoal for use on an open hearth. Its disinclination to burn is well recounted in local humour: four bags of coal from Durham or south Yorkshire reputedly being needed to set one bag of moor coal alight.

# 8 **Houses, roads and railways**

No examples of the everyday houses contemporary with the monasteries, castles and Royal Forest survive in the park. Simple wooden and thatch buildings perished or were replaced when worn out. But with greater use of stone the tendency increased to alter or extend, rather than totally demolish buildings.

Spout House, also known as the Sun Inn, Bilsdale, is one of the oldest cottages in the park. Built about 1550 on the site of an earlier building, it was initially a farm tenant's house. Situated alongside the Helmsley to Stokesley road its occupiers in the early eighteenth century seized the opportunity to take on a second job. In 1714 Spout House was licensed as an inn. And so it remained, part farmhouse, part public house, until the shutters came down for the last time in 1914 when the thriving business moved across the yard into the New Sun Inn.

Spout House, also known as the Sun Inn, is one of the oldest buildings in the park.

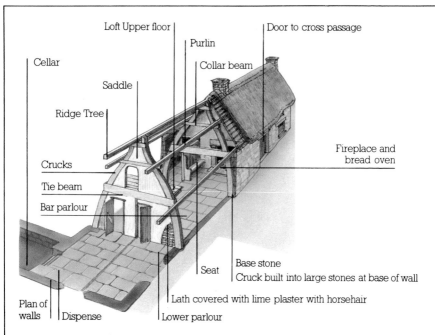

Loft Upper floor | Door to cross passage
Purlin
Cellar | Collar beam
Saddle
Ridge Tree
Fireplace and bread oven
Crucks
Tie beam
Bar parlour
Base stone
Seat | Cruck built into large stones at base of wall
Plan of walls | Dispense | Lath covered with lime plaster with horsehair
Lower parlour

The interior of Spout House.

Time stood still for Spout House. Even the furnishings were left. Over the years the building and its former life were all but forgotten, though its oven continued to be used for baking and the fire for heating water until the end of the Second World War.

By 1979 the building needed urgent attention to prevent it from falling into complete ruin. In an enterprising move the National Park Committee rented the property and financed renovation using traditional materials. The scheme retained the original fittings and furnishings to preserve the atmosphere of Spout House the day 'time' was called seventy years ago.

There is a strong unity of style within buildings throughout the region. Locally quarried sandstone in the north, limestone in the south and red clay pantiles for roofs, introduced to replace thatch in the late eighteenth century, are used extensively: a character which the National Park Committee strives to maintain through the planning procedures.

Many buildings retain features extending back over several centuries but the best perspective of old houses is to be gained in the attractive surroundings of Ryedale Folk Museum in Hutton-le-Hole. Here important examples of traditional buildings have been painstakingly removed piece by piece from their original sites and re-erected to their former configuration within a tasteful 'Folk Park'. As important as the houses are the 'Knick Knacks', agricultural equipment and tools of

A sixteenth-century manor house faithfully rebuilt in the grounds of Ryedale Folk Museum, Hutton-le-Hole.

everyday life in the museum's collections. Combined they are an illuminating insight into life-styles of the past. It is then up to the visitor to transpose a mental picture on to the villages and farms of the moors and dales.

A single-roomed crofter's cottage, constructed from archaeological and historical evidence, represents an ordinary thirteenth-century village house. The high roof helped to counteract the effects of a fire without a chimney: smoke wafted up into the roof and out through the thatch! The lack of a chimney must have rendered its occupants similar to kippers and the criss-cross wooden lattice-work windows – a forerunner of glass – leave plenty of room to speculate on their efficiency at keeping out the rain, birds and animals.

Three other delightful cruck-framed houses, a yeoman's home from Stang End, Danby, an eighteenth-century cottage, and a beautiful early seventeenth-century manor house, along with a variety of agricultural buildings, an early iron foundry and an Elizabethan glass furnace also stand in the grounds.

Discovered in Rosedale by Raymond Hayes, a local archaeologist, the furnace is a unique and important example of the type which was introduced into this country by French and Flemish glassworkers during the reign of Queen Elizabeth I.

Ever since the first people arrived in the North York Moors in prehistoric times economics have shaped the pattern of communities, land use, routes and methods of communications. The geology and climate dictated the potential, but its realization has been firmly bedded in the forces of supply and demand.

Tucked into the mouth of Roxby Beck, Staithes is one of the few places along the national park's coast where a fishing settlement has developed.

By the thirteenth century most of the villages of the park had already been long established. Exceptions were the handful along the coast. Sandsend is first mentioned in historic records in 1254; Runswick Bay in 1273; Staithes, a picturesque village at the mouth of Roxby Beck, in 1415, and the popular Robin Hood's Bay in the sixteenth century.

The region has always tended to turn its back on the sea. Had the coast been more accessible this might not have been the case. But natural impediments of rugged cliffs with few access points to the shore left little scope for development. These difficulties were compounded by the physical obstacle the moors presented to communication to and from the coast. There is much truth in the old saying 'There's only one road to Whitby, and that's by the sea'.

As trade expanded after the Dissolution of the monasteries, trains of thirty or forty packhorses were commonplace, working their way back and forth across the moors. Narrow stone-flagged pannier-ways provided a network of efficient commercial routes for the transport of coal, charcoal, ironstone, lime, wool and cloth in wet or dry conditions. This was in stark contrast to the state of the roads. They were an appalling mess; rough, deeply rutted and frequently impassable quagmires.

Where pannier-ways crossed infant streams, larger and deeper flat slabs were used as small bridges. In Eskdale six medieval bow-bridges took packhorse routes over the River Esk. Three, at Castleton, Danby and Briggswath, have been demolished. Hunters Sty at Westerdale, and Beggars Bridge at Glaisdale, are now bypassed, leaving only Duck Bridge still in everyday use. Its under seven-foot roadway and sharp hump require precise judgement of a vehicle's width. Built in 1396 it was reconstructed in 1726 by George Duck, of Danby Lodge (now The Moors Centre), after whom it is named. The coat of arms of the de Nevilles of Danby Castle is discernible on the parapet. It is to be hoped that no replacement is ever constructed alongside it, for Duck Bridge's isolation emphasizes the graceful sweep of its single arch.

Droving – the movement, often of large numbers of animals – needed wider tracks. The Hambleton Drove Road forms part of an ancient highway running from Scotland to the south and east of England. Along it cattle from Scotland were brought to the markets at Malton and York. Other animals

Duck Bridge, a medieval packhorse bridge spans the River Esk below Danby Castle.

and even turkeys were also driven along it.

From crossing the Tees at Yarm, the road first enters the park near Swainby before climbing steeply into the moors at Scarth Nick near Sheepwash. Having followed the high ground along the Hambleton Hills to Sutton Bank, it descends to Oldstead and then to Coxwold and on south.

Below Sutton Bank its route is no longer easily distinguishable, though through the park it is followed by the Cleveland Way.

A famous painting by Sir Edwin Landseer (*c.* 1830), 'The Drovers Departure for the South, Scene in the Grampians', captures the romantic image associated with the drovers. It gives a fair idea of the mobile menagerie droving must have been, though the romantic scene disguises the harsh reality of life on the road.

Farming settlements in the park evolved in different ways depending on the predominant type of agriculture. Nucleated villages – communities where houses are grouped closely together – such as in the Tabular Hills, are a sign of historical dependence on arable crop production. Work in the communal open fields often required group efforts to make economic sense of many jobs in the farming year. For example, an ox-team for ploughing might be made up of animals belonging to several households. Without this co-operation the

'The Drovers Departure for the South, Scene in the Grampians', by Sir Edwin Landseer *c.*1830.

task would have been beyond the resources of each individual.

Fragmented settlements in the dales are associated with pastoral farming. Animals grazing in permanent pastures, in woodlands, or on the moor did not require the same collective efforts. Consequently, isolated homesteads became established where they were most needed – near to flocks and herds.

Villages of clustered dwellings in agricultural areas of north-west Europe are a sign of historic dependence on arable farming.

Village lands were usually worked on a two- or three-field system. These open fields were split into furlongs and within each, households held separate strips of land. The two-field system was used on poorer soils, one field lying fallow every year. On better soils the three-field system allowed land to be rested every third year.

Not everyone in the village had the same rights. Some only possessed common grazing on the pastures and moors. Many households still hold these ancient rights, though often they are no longer exercised. .

By-laws, set by the manorial court, within whose boundaries the village lay, governed the use of the open fields. The rules were enforced by a by-law man, who ensured they were worked and stocked at correct levels in accordance with the rules. By-laws also included non-agricultural responsibilities, such as upkeep of certain fences, bridges and ditches.

The historic manorial courts have long since disappeared from most places in the country. However, thirty-one still exist, of which four – Whitbylaith, Fyling, Spaunton and Danby – are in the North York Moors. Every year the Danby Court

Leet Jury convenes in a room at Danby Castle to assess the fines (rents) to be levied on use of common land by the inhabitants of the manor. Even a muck heap placed outside a garden wall on the common would attract a nominal yearly fine. It is a colourful tradition and an effective way of preventing unscrupulous enclosure of common land. Around Danby and Glaisdale notices such as 'No Dumping' are signed 'by order Danby Court Leet'.

No-one really knows when many of the complicated and unwieldy open fields were enclosed and apportioned to individuals. Exchanges to rationalize the large number of small parcels of land into composite units had been taking place for some time before private parliamentary Acts statutorily enclosed them. Under the Acts, land and common-right holders were allotted new areas commensurate with, or in lieu of, their previous rights and holdings.

Allotment was sometimes achieved by agreement, but this was often difficult. One need only consider the proportion of twentieth-century litigation connected with boundary disputes to imagine the friction and ferocity of argument which wholesale reorganization would generate.

Acts of Parliament passed between the mid-eighteenth and mid-nineteenth centuries enclosed open fields, pastures, commons, moors and wastes in thirty-five parishes. The earliest at Faceby in 1748 enclosed 1,027 acres, and one of the last at Lockton and Saltergate Moor in 1872 enclosed 2,894 acres. Frequently the poorest land on the hilltops was awarded to the lord of the manor as a grouse moor. However some places have never been enclosed. Many areas of the moors are therefore technically still commons.

Fields were delineated by thorn hedges, or drystone walls. Where these were set by Parliamentary Acts, the boundaries tended to be straight and geometrical. Those enclosed piece-meal by agreement took on the more natural pattern of the preceding curved strips.

Agriculture always has been and still is the main industry of the region, despite its ups and downs and the appearance of other industries from time to time. 'Reaping and sowing' so they say 'have seen Empires in and out'. However, in the last three hundred years mining, quarrying, forestry and latterly tourism, have had an effect on the economy and settlement of the area. Their role has been

Even today some country roads through the moors are still rough, unmade tracks.

greatly influenced by the phenomenon of transport.

Until the fifteenth and sixteenth centuries wheeled traffic was rare. If you wanted to go anywhere you either walked or travelled on horseback. In 1555, Parliament passed a Highways Act to improve generally the standard of roads. This required parishes, not just landowners, to take a responsibility for their upkeep. The work was supposed to be carried out by parishioners, but little seems to have been achieved, except occasional construction of paved ways alongside difficult tracks, perhaps similar to that beside the Ainthorpe road near Duck Bridge.

Although communications were improving – a postal service was introduced between major towns in England during the sixteenth century – roads generally were still very poor two hundred years later. Their condition stifled trade everywhere.

Parliament's answer was the turnpike, built by private interests and used by the public on payment of tolls to cover the cost of construction. The trustees of 'Turnpike Trusts' were usually local landowners and merchants who would benefit from an improvement in transportation. The public was not always enthusiastic: main roads were improved, but the way was no longer free.

A turnpike connecting Whitby with the interior crossed the moors to Pickering about 1759. Thirty years later this route carried the first stage-coach services to York. A year after that another service commenced to Sunderland by a westerly route. The age of public transport had been born, but at an astronomical price. A thirty-five-mile journey in 1814 between Whitby and Stockton cost fourteen shillings if you travelled on the outside of the coach and twenty shillings if you sat inside. Coach services were susceptible to the vagaries of moorland weather, especially in winter, as road travel is still affected to this day. They were uncomfortable, unreliable and sometimes dangerous.

During the 1700s, canal systems developed widely in England, providing an easy means to transport large quantities of goods. With Whitby keen to stimulate trade by improving communications inland, proposals were made in 1793 to construct a canal along the Esk Valley, over the moors near Goathland, and down Newtondale to Pickering.

Rising by numerous locks to an altitude of over 500 ft (152 m), the canal would have been a considerable undertaking. After a detailed survey, not surprisingly, it was abandoned as impracticable. This was only a temporary set-back. In the early nineteenth century Whitby had other options . . .!

'This is the Age of the Train', a well used British Rail slogan of the 1980s came, in reality, over a century too late. The true age of the train arrived in the North York Moors, as elsewhere, long ago. Firstly during the railway boom of the 1830s and 40s, then during the mining expansion and finally with the explosion of popular excursions to the coast in the early part of this century. At York station a fine tile map of the North Eastern network in 1923 makes a depressing statement about the lack of lines today. Many places joined by routes on the map, such as Ravenscar, Sandsend, Hayburn Wyke and Robin Hood's Bay, have not seen a train for more than twenty years at the time of writing.

The railway era began with the new Stockton to Darlington railway in 1825. Five years later an eight-mile extension took the line to Middlesbrough where there was a harbour, but at that time no town; building of houses only commenced after the railway opened.

The elders of Whitby were not slow to recognize an opportunity when they saw one. Accordingly,

A historic London and
North Eastern railway tile
map in York station
depicts the rail network
as it was in 1923.

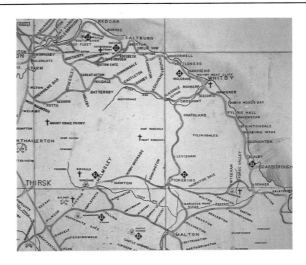

discussions took place with George Stephenson, the
engineer, about the best route to bring a railway to
the town. Stephenson carried out a detailed
cost/benefit analysis of two potential lines, one along
the Esk Valley from Stockton and the other over the
moors to Pickering. The commercial objectives
were the transport of good-quality coal from the
Durham coalfields to Whitby and, in the case of the
second option, transport of coal from Whitby to the
Pickering, Helmsley and Malton area. Stephenson
concluded that an Esk Valley line could not compete
with the existing shipment of coal by the Stockton
and Darlington railway to Middlesbrough, then by
boat to Whitby. On the other hand he estimated it
could be transported from Whitby to Pickering for
two shillings to three shillings per ton less than
inferior coal by different methods from elsewhere.

Construction of the Whitby and Pickering railway
presented certain difficulties. Crossing Fen Bog
required the sinking of large numbers of hurdles
covered with cut heather, turfs and larger timber to
make a more substantial foundation. At Beck Hole a
steep hill out of the valley of the Murk Esk to
Goathland was too great for normal working.
Carriages and wagons had to be raised and
lowered up and down the incline by wire rope.

To begin with, the line operated as a horse-drawn
tramway: it had not been thought potentially
profitable enough to justify steam locomotives. The
original carriages were open wagons and stage-
coaches on railway wheels. People were carried
inside and on the top.

A vital test for the railway came when heavy snow fell across the moors in December 1836. Sceptics were sure the trains wouldn't cope. But they did, with barely a hold-up. The doubters were silenced and the railway had come to stay – for a while at least.

In the early days, counterbalancing water-filled tanks on wheels worked carriages up and down Beck Hole incline. After a few years this system was abandoned in favour of a steam winding engine housed in a building at the top.

Until 1845, when an extension linked Pickering with the York and Scarborough line at Rillington, the Whitby and Pickering railway ran in isolation. During the intervening period stage-coaches connected with Malton and York. The accounts of the York to Whitby stage-coach for 1843 show a proportion of its income as payable to the railway, where the coach journey was now completed by train.

During the two years after the construction of the Rillington extension the line, which had been purchased by George Hudson, 'The Railway King', in 1845 was upgraded to double track and for through-working by steam locomotives. This required, amongst other things, a new and larger tunnel at Grosmont. The original horse-tunnel, with its turreted entrances, was retained as a footway to cottages and more recently sidings and sheds.

On the basis that something sooner or later goes

Beck Hole, at the foot of the old rope-worked railway incline, lies alongside the route of the Goathland to Grosmont Historical Railway Trail.

wrong with everything, the rope-worked incline presented a prime subject for disaster. On 10 February 1864 it came. The engine of the last train from Malton had been uncoupled and run around to the back of the carriages at the incline top. Gently it shunted them over the brow on to the brake-van attached to the winding-engine rope. Slack caused the rope to whip and snap where previously it had been run over and damaged. The brake-van and carriages plummeted downhill; there were no wheel brakes. Metal shoes lowered on to the track from the brake-van were the only means of slowing the train. These lifted the brake-van wheels off the track, leaving its weight and friction theoretically to do the rest! But one of the shoes broke. In the following moments the van and carriages careered from the rails and overturned; two people died and thirteen were injured.

The accident hastened the completion of a deviation line in 1865 to avoid the rope-worked system. It also speeded-up the introduction of coupled wheel-brakes on carriages!

With the new section complete, locomotives could haul through-trains from Whitby to Pickering, York and beyond. Beck Hole spur to the foot of the old incline remained open for tourist excursions until the First World War. The disused bed of the incline forms an important section of the Grosmont to Goathland Historical Railway Trail.

Three other railways followed to join Whitby with the rest of the country. In 1865 engineers completed the 'Esk Valley' line surmounting numerous problems to bridge meandering rivers seventeen times between Kildale and Grosmont, where it connected with the existing Pickering line. The 'Whitby–Loftus' completed the coastal link with Middlesbrough, the first section of which had been opened to Redcar by the famous engine 'Locomotion' in 1846. The main-line railway of East Cleveland united numerous branches and subsidiary lines servicing the iron mines of the area. Finally, in 1885 the 'Scarborough–Whitby' completed the passenger network. This spectacular twenty-one-mile route took thirteen years to build compared with the single year for the forty miles from York to Scarborough.

Trains brought tourists. Scenic lines, especially along the coast where deep gullies and valleys were crossed by high viaducts, were very popular. In the six years from 1895 to 1901 passenger numbers increased by forty per cent. They continued to rise until the beginning of the First World War, when not unexpectedly the traffic slumped.

The railways also attracted the speculator and his dreams. Centred on Ravenscar station, in the 1890s the Peak Estate Company planned a wholly new seaside resort. Roads, water supply and drains were laid and over 1,500 plots offered for sale. But the idea never caught on. Few buildings were constructed and the phantom 'Marine Esplanade', 'Hammond' and 'Arnold' roads of the ill conceived plans are now lost somewhere beneath the clifftop turf. No wonder the scheme failed. With high, steep cliffs, a rocky foreshore and a frequently windy, or mist-shrouded location it wasn't exactly the Victorian beach-goers' idea of heaven.

After the First World War tourist traffic picked up, reaching a peak in the 1930s. Again war brought it to an end. This time when hostilities ceased the railway did not recover. Equipment had become run down and by the 1950s 'The Age of the Train' was turning inexorably to 'The age of the private motor car'.

In 1958 the Whitby–Loftus line closed, followed by Scarborough–Whitby and Whitby–Pickering under the 'Beeching Axe' of 1965. Of the operational railways only the Esk Valley line has survived. But the 'ugly birds' of closure are frequently seen gathering in the trees. Perhaps its saviour so far has been the dependence of valley children on the railway to get to school in Whitby, especially in winter when roads are often impassable, icy and dangerous. It is a wonderfully attractive route and a good way to visit the national park.

Along the coast, sections of old track bed now form part of the Cleveland Way long-distance footpath and a concessionary footpath owned by Scarborough Borough Council. The flat surface makes for a comfortable walk through dramatic coastal scenery.

The Whitby and Pickering railway, however, lives again. Negotiations between the North York Moors Historical Railway Trust and British Rail culminated in the re-opening in stages of eighteen miles from Grosmont to Pickering as a privately run railway between 1968 and 1973.

From the shoulder of Newtondale those with fond recollections of the past can once again relive the experience of a distant train thumping out plumes of smoke and steam. At stations there is that special smell; the heat of the fire and the glistening of

Moorsrail, the North York Moors Historical Railway, is one of the longest private lines in the country. From Easter to October steam and diesel services are operated between Pickering and Grosmont.

golden grease. And for those to whom steam trains in everyday use exist only in books, there are the added opportunities to get a first speck of soot in an eye or to be covered with smuts at the trackside. These are the things steam engines were made of – missed entirely in a rail museum.

# 9 Agriculture and the industrial scene

At the same time as improvements in transport during the eighteenth and nineteenth centuries, rapid changes occurred on the moors when the jet, alum and iron industries blossomed and reached their peak.

Jet, the oldest extractive industry, dates from the Bronze Age. Traditionally pieces washed from the cliffs in the Whitby area were collected and worked into ornaments and jewellery. Victorian ladies, with a disposition for lengthy mourning and wearing black, made it a popular and much sought-after stone. To cater for the demand small mines burrowed into coastal cliffs and many dale sides, where lines of small spoil-heaps mark the jet outcrop. Inferior imported jet and changes in fashion, coupled with increased difficulty of supply, saw the once thriving industry decline. However it did not disappear entirely and modern-day jet workers in Whitby Old Town still find a market with visitors and the jewellery trade.

Jet and sea coal washed up on the beach are difficult to tell apart. Rubbing them against a stone shows up the difference: coal leaves a black mark, whereas jet leaves brown.

The prospect of Middlesbrough from the summit of Roseberry Topping is one of an enormous industrial area where complex structures of gantries, pressure vessels, piping and chimneys produce all manner of chemical products.

Twelve miles away at Spring Bank, Guisborough, and a far cry from the paraphernalia of Teesside, the first chemical industry in the country began about 1600.

Alum shale, quarried from Liassic rocks, was processed to produce alum, an important chemical used in the dyeing industry to fix colour. For the next 250 years vast quantities of the shale were extracted from numerous quarries stretching from Thimbleby to Saltburn, then round the coast to Ravenscar.

The lengthy process to produce alum crystals employed a peculiar assortment of materials – human urine, seaweed, wood and coal, as well as

From Easby Moor the lights of urban and industrial Teesside silhouette Roseberry Topping at night.

large quantities of alum shale.

Piled on to layers of brushwood and encased in wet clay, the shale formed huge mounds up to 200 feet long and wide and 100 feet high. Once fired, watering dampened the rate of burning. Often this lasted for many months and sometimes for longer than a year, reducing the mound to as little as half its original size. The brick-red coloured ash was then washed to dissolve the required chemicals and the resultant liquid transferred to a 'Boyling House'. The residue, dug out of the washing pits and dumped nearby, formed the pink spoil heaps, so closely associated with old alum workings, such as Carlton Bank, Kettleness, Sandsend Ness and Old Peak Ravenscar.

In the 'Boyling House' kelp (seaweed) was mixed with the liquid, which was then transferred to a settling tank, then scooped into a cooler where twenty gallons or more of urine were added. By yet another series of steps evaporation at last produced alum crystals. Three tons of alum was reckoned to be a reasonable production from 100 tons of shale, though contemporary accounts of alum workers suggest that often 100–130 tons of shale produced only one ton of crystals. With such poor return, weight for weight, it is understandable why most processing occurred adjacent to the quarry site.

Two things sounded the death knell for the Cleveland alum industry. Peter Spence, who invented a cheaper processing method using coal-

waste shales, started production at Goole in 1855. One year later synthetic dyes, which did not need fixing, were discovered. Boulby, the last works to close, struggled on for fifteen years, but the industry was already dead.

Old quarry workings amongst coastal cliffs north west of Staithes.

As one industry vanished, so another arose. Iron had begun to move into full swing.

Following the collapse of local iron-working in the mid-seventeenth century through lack of charcoal, amongst other things, foreign iron dominated the market for 100 years. Only when coke was discovered as a suitable fuel for blast furnaces in the mid-eighteenth century did the industry begin to pick up.

From about 1745 supplies of iron nodules washed from the cliffs and gathered from the shore at Robin Hood's Bay were shipped to furnaces on the Wear at Chester-le-Street. By 1800 they were also collected from the shore at Saltburn and Scarborough. However, this 'harvesting' could not meet the demand and iron was then quarried from the outcrops on the beach. In 1838 at Staithes these were worked between the tides.

The coming of the railways stimulated the iron industry in more ways than one. They provided an efficient means of transport. Equally important the railways themselves required large quantities of iron and steel for track, locomotive and rolling stock. But vitally for this region new ironstone measures of workable quality were discovered in Liassic rocks during excavation of the Whitby and Pickering railway tunnel at Grosmont in 1835. Within a year the first mine had opened, the ore being transported by train to Whitby and then by ship to furnaces on the Tyne. This gave the railway a welcome boost.

This was only a beginning. Soon the seams had been traced to the coast and across the Cleveland escarpment. Over the moors in Rosedale, new interest in ironstone saw samples sent to Durham for trial smelting.

Altogether more than eighty iron mines opened in the region. Most were drift mines, cut horizontally into the sides of hills, though some were shafts and a few were beach workings and quarries. Of the total over half lay within the park. The remainder, spread within an area bounded by Loftus, Redcar, Eston and Guisborough, eventually formed the main core of the Cleveland iron-mining industry.

The mines in the moors were concentrated in several areas: Lower Eskdale, especially around Grosmont and Glaisdale; the Cleveland escarpment above Guisborough; Rosedale, and along the coast. Small groups of isolated mines were worked near Swainby, Kildale and halfway up Roseberry Topping.

Evidence of old workings are plentiful – scars where drifts cut into slopes, buildings, traces of rail track beds and terraces of miners' cottages, such as Gribdale Terrace, Great Ayton, New Row, Kildale and several rows in Rosedale.

About 1856 rocks from an outcrop on Hollins Farm near Rosedale Abbey were analysed. Lightning frequently struck the outcrop, giving rise to the local belief that the devil or treasure lay buried within it. No-one found the devil, but analysis did discover a kind of treasure: the rocks were valuable, high grade, magnetic ironstone. Needless to say the outcrop which previously had been quarried and wasted as a roadstone was soon rapidly mined away.

For several years ore from Hollins mine was transported through Cropton to the railway at Pickering, though the going proved difficult on the poor roads. In 1861 the extension of a branch line from Battersby to Rosedale Bank Top by the North Eastern railway overcame the problem. At Ingleby Incline the track climbed diagonally up the escarpment, rising nearly 700 feet from the Cleveland plain to the moor in little more than one mile. From the summit of the incline it crossed eleven miles of open moor to Rosedale Bank Top. At the terminus a steep tramway drew ores up from the mines in the valley to calcinating kilns. Here the rock was 'roasted' to burn off moisture and reduce

its weight, before transport to the blast furnaces on Teesside. This lessened transport costs as well as the royalty payment per ton.

The Rosedale mines railway track passed under the Hutton-le-Hole to Castleton road just south of the Lion Inn on Blakey Rigg. The bridge arch is now blocked, but the west parapet beside the road junction to Farndale and the cutting are still obvious.

At Blakey, in 1865 an additional four-and-three-quarter-mile long branch line opened, following the contour round the head of the dale to High Baring and the Rosedale East mines which started operation that year. Another three-quarter-mile spur cut into the east side of Farndale in 1873 where an unsuccessful attempt was made to find a continuation of the rich magnetic ironstone seam.

Blakey Junction, situated about 100 yards from the road, became a small hamlet. Only a few bricks now remain to mark where its families lived and worked: the last house being demolished in 1955. Immediately opposite across the valley the 'ancient temple' quality of the ruined East mines calcinating kilns make a fitting shrine to the extraordinary scenes in Rosedale over a century ago.

The changes were dramatic, as witnessed in an

A terrace of old miners' cottages below Roseberry Topping provides a reminder of the days when the moors was an iron-mining area.

Derelict calcinating kilns in which the ironstone from Rosedale East mines was roasted.

extract from a letter sent on 12 March 1869 by an inhabitant to relatives who had moved to America:

'If you had to see Rosedale now you would hardly know it, it is very nearly turned inside out since you were here. There are railroads both sides of the Dale now and two great big ironstone kilns to burn iron-stone. The ground is hollow for many a mile underground and houses built in all directions. It's like a little city now but is a regular slaughter place. Both men and horses are getting killed and lamed every day. When I am writing this letter they are carrying a man home past our house either killed or badly hurt . . . meat is very dear – there is no sort of meat under 8d the lb and bacon is 10d, ham 1/–, eggs 16 for a shilling and butter 1/6 per lb – so we are coming to America, my husband is sick of Rosedale.'

The alterations to the agricultural community, brought by mining were indeed immense. In 1851 the total population of Rosedale was 558. At the peak of the mining in 1871 it had risen to 2,839, but declined to 702 in 1881, when the mines had been shut for two years following the collapse of the then owners, Rosedale and Ferryhill Mining Company.

Ruined cottages, once homes to members of Rosedale's thriving mining community.

By 1891 the population had risen again to over 1,300, though by now the west mines had already ceased production: the numbers never again reached previous levels.

Increasing costs and finally the General Strike of 1926 killed Rosedale mines. For one or two years afterwards slag from below the calcinating kilns, which was rich in iron oxide, continued to be removed to Teesside for processing. This task completed, the railway engines were lowered down the Ingleby Incline, and the line closed in 1929. By 1931 the population had fallen to 962 and in the 1960s to 286 – Rosedale had reverted to a peaceful rural scene.

The other mines and the few blast furnaces which had been built to smelt ore at Runswick Bay, Beck Hole, Grosmont and Glaisdale, generally fared worse.

After the discovery of substantial workable measures in the Eston Hills near Middlesbrough in 1850, numerous new furnaces were constructed on Teesside. It was the Eston mines which gave real impetus to the Teesside iron industry.

The furnaces at Runswick Bay and Beck Hole were commercially ill conceived, inadequately constructed and soon failed. Those at Glaisdale didn't do much better. However Grosmont's were more successful, though even they could not compete with large-scale operations around the Tees. In the 1880s, for one reason or another, iron smelting in the moors ceased.

Of more than forty sites of iron-mining ventures within the park, only Sherriff's Pit, Rosedale;

Rosedale East; Slapewath; Eskdale and Grinkle survived into the twentieth century.

One or two new mines opened between 1900 and 1910, but by 1934, when Boulby and Grinkle closed, the others had all gone too. Beyond the park, mining in East Cleveland continued for another thirty years

Port Mulgrave was created specially to cater for the shipment of ore from the iron mines of East Cleveland.

until the early 1960s. Nothing is forever. Like the boom days of the monastic sheep flocks, the jet and alum industries at their height and the railways which came and went in 100 years, iron's 'day was done' too.

Bombardment of the East Coast by the German navy during the First World War knocked bits off Whitby Abbey and blew holes in Scarborough Castle, as well as causing considerable damage to the towns. Direct action certainly left a mark, but the indirect results of war on the landscape were to be far wider reaching.

Disafforestation, a progressive problem since medieval times, became a serious strategic issue. Blockading of ports by enemy submarines cut off supplies of imported timber, amongst other commodities and raw materials. Royal Navy warships and merchant vessels were powered by coal-fired boilers; industry needed coal and wood; and the mines needed wooden pit-props in order to work the coal. Further felling supplied this pressing need.

After the war, the Government, recognizing the shortage, established the Forestry Commission. Its brief was simple: to make good, with urgency, the losses of woodland and to increase forests against future requirements. The Commission sought to acquire the cheapest suitable land. Often this meant uplands, such as the North York Moors, where the agricultural value, and hence the price, was relatively low. By 1921, two years after the Commission's inception, tree planting had begun at Dalby, near Thornton Dale.

Similar land acquisition and planting followed the Second World War. In forests established before 1950 Scots pine predominated, though this was superseded by lodgepole pine as planting moved on to higher, wetter ground. More recently, with improved cultivation techniques, Sitka spruce has become the most widely planted tree. Over fifty per cent of the present forest stock comprises different species of pines; twenty-six per cent various spruces; nineteen per cent larches and six per cent other conifers. About four per cent are hardwoods, mainly oak, beech and sycamore.

The North York Moors Forest District, administered from Pickering, manages over 50,000 acres of trees. Bar one isolated block in the Howardian Hills, the entire holding lies within the national park where Dalby and Cropton form the largest upland heath forests in England. Employing nearly 150 people, the management district handles all stages of the forest cycle, from the tree nursery at Wykeham – supplying millions of saplings – to thinning, felling, removal, cultivation and replanting. However about half the timber is sold standing and extracted by timber merchants and contractors.

First-time planting of the Commission's holdings is virtually complete at time of writing and the emphasis of management has now shifted to harvesting mature timber, cultivation and re-planting of felled sites. Conifer forest brought perhaps the most rapid visual change since the Ice Age; equally its removal also has a sudden impact. To minimize this, felling is carefully planned, using adjacent trees as a screen. No two neighbouring sections of the forest are felled at the same time and only when new stock has grown sufficiently are trees removed from adjoining areas. Gone from the planners' thinking are the enormous geometric blocks which swept with functional rigidity across the terrain. Forest design now takes account of the natural contours and features of the land. The Forestry Commission's prime duty is still to supply timber, but the public which once demanded strategic supplies now seeks something more: recreation, landscape and wildlife conservation are all embodied within the management of the trees.

Seventy per cent of the timber produced is sold for sawlogs, ten per cent for pulp and the remainder as poles and for miscellaneous uses such as firewood and box wood. There is even a chance that the cereal packet on your breakfast table once stood in a remote place on the North York Moors before the tree was reduced to pulp in paper and cardboard mills.

It does not take an expert to recognize different types of agriculture within the park: intensive arable farming across the free-draining and inherently fertile Tabular Hills; mixed farming on the boulder clays along the coast; pastoral farming in the dales, with traditional sheep grazing on the open sandstone moorland.

Geographically the North York Moors could be said to begin where the ground starts to rise from the Vales of Pickering and York and the Cleveland Plain. But to the farmer they start where the limestones and boulder clays give way to the poorer sandstone soils. Agriculture on the southwards-sloping hills between Sutton Bank and Thornton Dale is to all intents and purposes an extension of the rich arable farming in the Vale of Pickering, whereas in the dales it is mainly geared to rearing animals and producing milk.

Historically cattle were run up to and even into the heather, bracken was cut for bedding and heavy reliance placed on the free-roaming sheep flocks; farmers scratched a living wherever they could. With the advent of modern fertilizers, grass fields in the valleys could be improved. This produced better grazing, reducing dependence on the less productive hills.

The relevance of different crops and land uses are difficult for a non-farmer to appreciate. To help visitors understand the complexities the National Park Authority established a farm trail on Forestry Commission property at May Beck, for which an excellent guide-book is available. The trail demonstrates the progression from arable or pasture in the valley bottoms to enclosed grassland (claimed from the moor) or open rough moorland. Fields close to the moor have a tendency to revert or succumb to bracken encroachment. Application of fertilizer and occasional ploughing and reseeding is therefore needed to retain the quality of the grazing. Pastoral agriculture in the dales is devoted to sheep and cattle rearing, both of which are supplied to lowland farms for fattening. Hay and silage are made, and most arable crops such as oats,

barley and turnips grown for winter animal feed. Dairy herds of black and white Friesian cattle are common in valley bottoms. And suckler herds, of hardy crossbred cows, each rearing its own calf, are often run with a Hereford or Charolais beef bull in the poorer higher pastures.

Traditional upland sheep farming stems directly from the practices introduced by the monasteries. The Swaledale is the most popular hill breed, although Scottish Blackface are favoured in some areas. These hardy sheep are run on the moors throughout the year, though most of the ewes are brought down from the hills for lambing in spring.

Today's farmers are no longer so dependent on hill flocks. Crossing traditional moorland sheep with less hardy breeds and rearing them in improved valley fields is frequently more rewarding. In recent years the number of flockmasters has declined and, with increased deaths especially of lambs on unfenced roads, many farmers seriously question whether moorland grazing is really worthwhile.

In late summer and early autumn sheep are rounded up. Those to be sold are brought to sheep sales, such as Glaisdale, Castleton and the Lion Inn at Blakey Rigg. A visit to these concentrations of

Typical moorland farm buildings, developed from the longhouse, in Little Fryup Dale.

Bransdale. The upper limit of the farmland in the valleys often coincides with the change in the underlying rocks from lias in the valley bottom to the sandstone with its poor soils above.

Harsh winter near
Hawnby.

local activity offers an infrequent opportunity to
sample the flavour of a farming community, which
for most of the year, like its sheep, is spread far and
wide amongst the hills.

Farming in the mid 1980s is going through
troubled times. With subsidies and quotas under
eternal discussion, and EEC ministers frantically
trying to manage surpluses or balance the books,
the hill farmer has become especially threatened by
the economic pressures of a competitive world.
Agricultural finance, specially defined agricultural
zones, incentives, subsidies and grants, are so
complex and liable to change on political whim that
it is pointless to describe them in a guide-book such
as this. Except perhaps to mention one – the upland
sheep subsidy, by which farmers receive a payment
from the government for every sheep they have;
without it there would be no sheep on the hills.

Autumn sheep sale.

# 10 **The pressures of modern times**

It is little short of amazing that while the nation pieced itself together after the Second World War, the Government had the will and vision to seek to protect the country's finest landscapes for future generations to enjoy. Against a background of rationing and economic exhaustion, the National Parks and Access to the Countryside Act received Royal Assent in 1949. In 1952 an order made under that Act designated the North York Moors as a national park. The decades which followed have been times of increasing social change with agricultural revolution, mass ownership of motor vehicles, international travel, increased leisure time, unemployment, the Cold War, the nuclear society and a spectacular spread of conservation ideals covering many facets of the countryside, especially wildlife; each in its own way is subtly, and sometimes not so subtly, manifest in the moorland scene.

In a résumé of transport in Yorkshire, Colin Speakman penned an excellent description of the motor car:

'A car is go where you want. A car is the whole family together cheaply and conveniently. A car is a little home on wheels. A car is freedom.'

The motor car certainly brought freedom to the upland farmer; no longer was living so remote. It brought freedom to millions of other people too. In 1939 there were two million or so cars on the road. By 1959 the number had passed four million. Then the graph climbed steeply, reaching ten million 'little homes on wheels' by the late 1960s and a phenomenal sixteen million twenty years later.

The public could now choose exactly where it wanted to go. No longer constrained by bus and railway routes and timetables, distant places became easily accessible within a day trip from home, or for a longer holiday. Some critics blame the national park for attracting large numbers of people to the moors. But they would have come to enjoy themselves anyway – and why not? It was the beautiful landscape, not the national park *per se* they sought, and the car gave them an easy means to do it.

'A car is freedom. But when twelve, twenty or even thirty million people have that freedom and all want to exercise it in similar places at a similar time, the result is a complete loss of freedom. It is a nightmare.'

Mercifully 'nightmare' levels of traffic are rare, except on the main Guisborough to Whitby and Thirsk to Scarborough roads during summer school-holiday weekends. The National Park Authority provides a convenient mechanism to monitor potential difficulties and where possible seek solutions in the interest of all concerned.

However, mobility has had other effects. Visitors came and liked what they saw. For those who could afford it second homes or holiday homes were an obvious progression. Some villages such as Robin Hood's Bay which thrived in the summer season turned to ghost towns in winter. In Eskdale, commuters could enjoy rural living yet travel easily by car to work in Teesside. House prices increased, placing them beyond the reach of many in the local

Women's Institute art class in Hutton-le-Hole.

community. Lack of available houses, made worse by a general drop in agricultural employment, saw village schools close and farming communities dwindle, as sons and daughters took jobs in towns, or moved outside the park to make their home. The private car also firmly hammered the nails into the coffins of many rural bus and train services.

Not everything which meets the eye fits the picture of the peaceful rural scene, though features which jar are few and far between. Superlatives, such as largest, biggest, smallest, are an irresistible attraction. But few people come to the moors to see the longest lift in Europe. Indeed it is quite difficult to imagine where such a lift might be.

Bilsdale BBC television transmitter mast is not the most beautiful of structures. Inside the slim pencil, conjured into a balancing act by a few guy-ropes, the service lift for engineers to maintain the aerials takes seven minutes to travel 930 ft (284 m) to the top.

All the major modern structures are visible from considerable distances. Standing on the site of the signalling station at Danby Beacon, occupied by a soldier and his wife during the Napoleonic Wars, the top of Bilsdale Mast prods the south-western sky fifteen miles away. Due north, Boulby potash mine chimney marks the deepest shaft in England, completed in 1973. Here potash is extracted from the Permian rocks over 3,750 ft (1,143 m) below the surface.

Between the Beacon and Boulby, Scaling Dam collects run-off from several local moors to provide an important water resource for Teesside and Boulby mine. Its overflow feeds Roxby Beck which

Boulby potash mine, the deepest shaft in Britain.

empties into the sea at Staithes. To the south east a signalling station of a different kind lies hunched on a hillside. Along with Thule in Greenland and Cape Clear, Alaska, the Royal Air Force's Fylingdales Early Warning Station forms part of the NATO defensive network. Its bizarre shape – three large domes known affectionately as 'The Golf Balls' – are by far the most obvious man-made feature in the park. Yet in a peculiar way, these mysterious buildings are not altogether offensive in their setting. However the Ministry of Defence is planning to convert them to a single pyramid. It will be interesting to see, as the conversion proceeds, whether there are complaints of aesthetic preference for the existing installation. Fylingdales, like Boulby, is an important employer of local people, especially from Whitby, in an area with a serious unemployment problem.

During the Second World War large sections of the moors were used as tank training areas. Today, other than Fylingdales, there is little military presence on the ground: in the air it is a totally different story!

Much of Britain, including the North York Moors, is used for low flying training. It is not unusual to see Tornados and Jaguars negotiating the hills and valleys at 500 mph, as low as 250 ft (80 m). The National Park Committee endeavours to encourage

Fylingdales Early Warning Station. The original hemispheres housing the radar equipment became a tourist attraction.

A United States Air Force plane sweeps round the Cleveland escarpment on a low-level sortie.

the Royal Air Force to find other areas in which to train. But realistically in a small island it is difficult to see what alternatives there can be. Complaints about 'bolts from the blue' of noise are regular, but these are tempered by the sentiments of at least one farmer:

> 'Yes, they're a nuisance – though I'm just glad they're ours!'

Not everyone finds the planes an intrusion. Jets, ripping through the air in steeply banked turns near the ground, are a free and thrilling display of raw power. An unpopular thing to admit? But thousands of ordinary people don't go to Battle of Britain air shows for nothing.

The aircraft are our age's medieval cannon, and Fylingdales Early Warning Station is simply a development from the stone defences of Pickering and Helmsley Castles. It does however seem very odd that while the weapons of war are exercised overhead, concern for the finer points of our wildlife and landscape has never been so great.

# 11 **Wildlife**

Cliff faces and the narrow strip of shore between high and low tides are the only natural places in the national park. Everywhere else has been affected by man to a greater or lesser degree. Whether by Mesolithic hunter, medieval charcoal worker, or the present-day hill farmer responding to the financial juggling of the EEC, all have played an integral part in the evolution of wildlife habitats in the park.

Remains of pre-Ice Age animals found in Kirkdale Cave included species no longer to be seen in the moors. Giant deer and straight-tusked elephant are totally extinct; brown bear, wolf, lion, and hyena survive in places abroad; and a few wild cat and polecat in other parts of Britain; whereas fox, badger and stoat still remain. Why are some extinct and not others? Why is the growl of the brown bear no longer heard on the wooded hillsides, nor the scream of the hyena across the valleys? The reasons for extinction are many: climatic changes, competition between species and disease can all play a part. But in recent times it has been mainly the influence of man.

European brown bear.

Brown bear had gone from the moors perhaps as long ago as Roman times, though certainly by the eleventh century; a formidable animal, it would not have been the easiest of companions for early man in the forest and was ruthlessly hunted. The last wolf, perhaps in the whole of England, was despatched near Pickering about 1650; in a predominantly sheep-farming district it was another unwelcome neighbour. Loss of habitat, disturbance, persecution or over-hunting have seen the reindeer, beaver and wild boar go the same way over the centuries. The region's last polecat was killed in the 1920s; pine marten disappeared in the late 1950s and the red squirrel, last seen in Duncombe Park near Helmsley, has not been recorded since 1975. Extinctions are by no means things of the past. Several species cling on literally by the skin of their teeth. The otter is on the brink, with only a tiny isolated population in the North York Moors, out of perhaps 200 animals in England and Wales. Nationally the merlin is in severe trouble, as are many species of bats.

It sounds a gloomy and sorry tale: But the losses and problems serve very well to concentrate the mind on the rich variety the moors still retain. Nothing can be taken for granted, not the wildlife, nor the historical landscape management on which so much of it depends.

Plants are the only things on Earth able to convert the sun's energy into food for other living things. They are the basic 'building blocks' on which all animals rely. The belt of limestone from Sutton Bank to Scarborough, which has suited farmer and forester over the centuries, also supports the greatest variety of wild plants. Conversely, poor acidic moorland soils are home to relatively few. In the sea the most familiar plants are seaweeds. Green seaweeds are common, though brown – the wracks and kelps – dominate the shallows and shore, and red seaweeds prefer shady or deeper places.

The sea is teeming with life, from microscopic phytoplankton – single-celled plants drifting with the current – to huge kelp beds. On open and weed-covered rocks, under boulders, and in pools, numerous animals, including whelks, starfish, crabs, and sponges occupy their own particular niches. In rock pools at Robin Hood's Bay, Staithes, Burniston and Ravenscar feeding barnacles and anemones, or small crustaceans sunning themselves, await the patient and inquisitive visitor. The abundant source of food attracts turnstone, oystercatcher and purple sandpiper, especially in winter. And on beaches dunlin, sanderling, redshank and perhaps the occasional bar-tailed godwit probe the tideline in search of small animals living in the wet sand.

Arctic tern;
common tern;
sandwich tern.

During late summer and early autumn sandwich, common and Arctic terns fly south towards their winter quarters off Africa or South America. Sometimes at Sandsend in the evening, after most visitors have gone, these 'sea-swallows' hover, then plunge into the water to catch small fish, or rest on the beach. The family car, parked at the roadside overlooking the sands, makes an excellent observation post. Some species, for example, herring gull, kittiwake and fulmar – a relative of the albatross, breed on coastal cliffs and the lumbering cormorant nests at their foot near Ravenscar. In winter, Arctic and great skuas pirate other sea birds' last meals, harassing them in dramatic chases until they 'throw-up'. Even with binoculars distant birds are difficult for the non-specialist to identify,

Kittiwake.

but large gleaming white gannets are easily picked out, diving into the water to catch their prey.

Eighteen miles south of the park the Royal Society for the Protection of Birds's Bempton Cliffs nature reserve offers an unparalleled opportunity to see vast numbers of sea birds at close quarters. The cliffs are a veritable city of guillemots, razorbills, gannets, puffins, kittiwakes and shags. At the edge the wall of noise and smell, blasting upwards on an on-shore wind at the height of the breeding season is something to behold.

Not all animals out to sea are birds. Very occasionally a dolphin or whale may pass by. However, grey seals, probably from the breeding colonies on the Farne Islands, off the Northumberland coast, regularly come close to shore.

Moorland is the dominant wildlife habitat of the North York Moors. Its 160 square miles form the largest continuous tract of heather in England and Wales. Ling, which blooms in late summer, is by far the most widespread plant. The less common, deep purple, bell heather and pale pink, cross-leaved heath both bloom a few weeks earlier. Patches of bright green bilberry clothe many banks; bracken smothers the moorland edge and in boggy hollows and wet flushes sphagnum moss and cotton grass are abundant. Insect-eating sundew grows both in bogs and on the permanently wet soils where infant streams emanate from these gigantic moorland sponges. Occasionally heath spotted orchid and the stout yellow-flowered bog asphodel bring dots of colour to the scene. And bog myrtle, bearing a passing resemblance to a low-growing willow, adds a touch of fragrance when bruised or crushed. An active ingredient of gale beer, it has helped refresh many a dry throat at haytime in the past.

Blanket peat spread thinly and widely across the moor sometimes attains considerable thickness in hollows and bogs. It is still cut for fuel in places. Near the Glaisdale to Rosedale Abbey road, workings reveal the depth of the accumulation.

For several hundred years the heather moor has been grazed by sheep and subsequently managed by regular burning for grouse shooting. Heather burning takes place in early spring or autumn when the ground is wet. These carefully controlled fires destroy old heather stems, but leave its roots, and the peat in which they grow, undamaged. Grouse feed on succulent new shoots which sprout from the fired ground and nest amongst the dense older

Bell heather.
Ling heather.

The tiny sundew obtains the nitrogen it needs from the bodies of insects which become trapped on its sticky leaves.

Rotational burning is the traditional method of managing the heather moor.

heather. Rotational burning on a ten- to fourteen-year cycle produces a patchwork of different-aged plants. As well as encouraging the red grouse it also suits several other species of birds too.

Grouse shooting can evoke strong views, but its importance to other wildlife should not be underestimated. Without the shooting interest owners might well seek alternative uses for their land as pasture or forest with a consequent loss for species dependent on open heather moor. During winter few birds other than the grouse remain on the exposed hills. Wandering gulls, or an occasional hen harrier and small migrating flocks of snow buntings, other than the ever hardy sheep, provide the only movement.

Spring brings dramatic change. Lapwing, curlew and golden plover, with redshank and snipe, meadow pipit and migrant wheatear, and ring ouzel return to their breeding grounds. Golden plover only nest in recently burnt areas. Lapwing will not tolerate tall heather, and snipe, curlew and redshank favour tussocks in or near wet flushes, or in old rough pastures. The lapwing with its long crest and broad black and white wings is a superb flyer, twisting and turning in display, or in defence of its nest and chicks. Frequently seen feeding in the short roadside turf, it is the best known moorland bird.

Sparrow-sized meadow pipits perform an unusual display flight called 'parachuting'. Firstly they fly up, then descend singing, with feet dangling, wings trembling and tail held high. A regular host to the cuckoo, meadow pipits are the main prey of the very rare merlin. Only exceedingly lucky visitors will catch sight of this small, darting falcon. But its close relative the kestrel is common along the moorland edge, where in late summer family groups hunt together, hovering in a line a few hundred yards apart.

Red grouse.

The kestrel feeds mainly on small mammals, but also insects and sometimes small birds and even reptiles. It has been known to carry off the venomous adder in its talons. Adders, which regularly bask in warm sunshine, pose little threat to human beings and soon glide into cover at the least disturbance. The rarer slow-worm, neither a snake nor worm, but a legless lizard, prefers the valley edge. Common lizards, the only other reptiles of the region, frequent banks on both open moorland and valley sides. Quick as lightning they dart in and out of drystone walls or bask in the sun on a warm rock or old tree stump.

Newts look like lizards, but are amphibians. Palmate newts, distinguished by their webbed feet, breed in some moorland ponds. The large,

Heather grows in the thin layer of peat which covers the rocky ground.

handsome, golden-ringed dragonfly usually associated with streams may even be encountered laying eggs in puddles on moorland tracks, whereas the turquoise and black aeshna dragonfly hunts its prey by water on both the high and the low ground.

Pride of place among moorland insects must go to the emperor moth. On sunny late April and May days, richly coloured males fly rapidly in search of females. Male emperor moths may possess one of the keenest sense of smell of any living thing. The larger, patterned grey female exudes an odour which males can detect with their feathery antennae, from over three miles away. Green and black emperor caterpillars feed on heather. Fully grown by mid-summer, they spin a bottle-shaped cocoon amongst the heather stems in which to pupate. A ring of outward-pointing fibres blocks the neck of the cocoon against insect intruders, but allows the newly hatched moth to emerge.

Large, hairy, rusty brown and black caterpillars of the northern eggar – another day-flying moth – wander some distance in search of a place to pupate. Their hairs contain an irritant which helps to protect them against predators: it is not advisable to pick them up!

Green hairstreak and small heath butterflies, common on the moor edge, have an infuriating habit of closing their wings instantly on landing, making it impossible to appreciate their colours. Male green hairstreaks are a beautiful iridescent green; the female, lustrous brown, and the small heath, a sandy orange.

Recent moorland research by Dr Roy Brown of North York Moors National Park Department produced some interesting results. Small mammals not readily associated with the heather moor occur widely. It is thought these may well be relict populations of mice, voles and shrews which once inhabited woodlands previously covering the hills.

Larger mammals are rarely encountered. Of them brown hare and rabbits are most likely to be seen. The ubiquitous fox is as much at home here as anywhere else and although badgers cross from valley to valley their setts are unlikely to be found far on to the moorland. Stoats and weasels are not uncommon near farm land, where they are most likely to be spotted crossing the road in front of the car.

Woodlands fall into two broad categories – broad-leaved and coniferous – though the wildlife

Female emperor moth.

importance of each varies depending on the wood's antiquity and species of trees it contains. An old over-mature plantation of native Scots pine is very different to a new plantation of introduced conifers. Similarly there is a considerable contrast between a young plantation of sycamore and an ancient mixed deciduous wood.

Almost all the ancient deciduous woodland, comprising less than five per cent of the national park, lies in the steep-sided valleys where rivers cut through the Tabular Hills; in the undulating lower Esk Dale; or along ravines leading to the sea. They have survived mainly where the terrain is too steep for agriculture and in spite of commercial trends to replant with conifers. Some sites have borne trees since forest first spread after the Ice Age, though they may have been felled or coppiced and allowed to regrow many times. The wild flowers of an ancient wood, especially on limestone, are dramatically different to both a new deciduous or a conifer plantation. Dog's mercury, bluebells, sanicle and moschatel – also known as five-faced bishop and town-hall clock – only occur where deciduous woodland has been established for a very long time.

Near Rievaulx, the rare green hellebore is one of the earliest plants to flower. Often associated with old monasteries, it may have been used by monks in a medicinal remedy for the treatment of leprosy. By mid-May the best of the mixed oak and ash woods are a carpet of wood anemones, violets, and primroses, with water and wood avens, wood sorrel and occasional early purple orchids. In the Kirkbymoorside district, false oxslip – a cowslip/primrose cross – is not uncommon. A few weeks later drifts of snow-white ramsons, also called wild garlic, sweep down hillsides under the new leaf canopy; their strong smell of onion carries on the wind, especially at night.

Toothwort, a leafless parasite on the roots of trees, particularly hazel, is perhaps the most curious plant of the region. Its old country name 'corpse flower' stems from a belief that the plant only grew where a corpse was buried. The name toothwort comes not from the pale pink, tissue-paper-like flowers, but from its roots which resemble a row of molar teeth.

Birdlife of ancient woods is equally rich. Green and great spotted woodpecker are more frequently heard than seen. Treecreeper are not uncommon and nuthatch are to be found occasionally in the southern half of the park. Summer visitors, including

Wood anemone or 'wind flower'.

Toothwort – a parasitic plant which grows on tree roots.

Nuthatch.

willow warbler, chiffchaff, and spotted flycatcher, are common, particularly along woodland edges. Redstart and blackcap occur widely and pied flycatcher nest in a few localities each year.

Woodland carparks are some of the best places to enjoy birds. In Forge Valley during winter and early spring, coal, blue, great and long-tailed tits, nuthatch, jay, great spotted woodpecker and the jackdaw are unusually tame.

Some wooded areas of the national park are a stronghold of the badger; fox are common and roe, fallow and even occasionally red deer are seen. Their fresh footprints are frequently identifiable on muddy paths.

Some people hate conifer forest, believing that the dark rows of trunks beneath a dense leaf canopy are the nearest thing to hell on earth. Others derive immense pleasure from the depth which vast areas of trees can bring to a landscape. There is no doubt that there is a certain magic about the endless forest, where civilization does not confront you round each bend. However, where conifers have replaced moorland, ancient deciduous woodland or grassland there is an inevitable and sometimes considerable loss of the wildlife dependent on those habitats. But conifer forest is a habitat in its own right, on which different species may equally depend.

At the turn of the last century roe deer were virtually extinct. Only about eighty family groups are thought to have been left in the entire country. Forestry Commission plantations were their salvation, to a point where they are now widespread and numerous. Crossbills and siskins nest in Dalby and Cropton Forests. In winter the siskin population increases with migrants from Scandinavia. Members of the tit family, especially coal and long-tailed tits, and the tiny goldcrest are common. Sparrowhawks breed in plantations and hunt through woodlands, along rides and across adjoining open ground.

Perhaps the greatest value of the conifer forest for wildlife in recent years has been for the nightjar. This nocturnal bird migrates from Africa. But many of the heaths where it used to nest have been destroyed. With removal of the first mature trees, nightjars have adopted clear-felled areas in which to breed. No-one who has heard the sound of a nightjar 'churring' at dusk will ever forget it. Delivered from the top of a silhouetted tree its song carries a mile or more on a still night, changing note

as the male turns his head from side to side. In folk-lore the nightjar, also known as lych fowl, is a bird of evil omen, said to embody the soul of a child which died unbaptized. If the omen doesn't deter the night-time walker then there is every chance of hearing its weird call flowing across the darkened landscape of Cropton and Dalby Forests.

Stretches of open water are sparse. Of these, most are man-made. Scaling Dam and Lockwood Beck Reservoirs alongside the Whitby to Guisborough road, near Castleton, are the most important. Here numerous wildfowl and wading birds pass through in autumn or over-winter. Without these artificial lakes there would be no similar winter habitat in the region for many species. Records at Scaling Dam include widgeon, pintail, dunlin and the rare red-necked grebe from eastern Europe.

Staindale Lake in Dalby Forest was created for visitors by the Forestry Commission. Set in attractive surroundings it is easily accessible, especially to the elderly and handicapped. Tufted duck, mallard and breeding Canada geese are resident, and other birds from woodland, streamside and open areas, such as grey wagtail, wren and chaffinch feed nearby.

Gormire Lake, the largest natural stretch of open water, can only be reached after a long walk. Sutton Bank nature trail winds down a steep escarpment through the Yorkshire Wildlife Trust's Garbutt Wood nature reserve to the waterside where tufted loosestrife blooms in summer and great crested grebe are sometimes present.

Two groups of rivers drain virtually the entire moorland: the 'Esk system' to the north, and the

Felled forestry plantations are an important breeding place for nightjars.

Herons suffer badly in severe winters when their food is locked under frozen streams and rivers.

'Derwent system' to the south. However, only the River Esk reaches an appreciable size collecting the streams from Westerdale, Danby Dale, Great and Little Fryup Dales and Glaisdale on its meander along the Esk Valley.

Rivers of the southern dales all leave the park separately, before uniting at various points across the Vale of Pickering to finally form the main stream of the Derwent at Rye Mouth three miles above Malton.

Alder, the natural waterside tree of the region, lines most banks, tracing river courses through farmland in valley bottoms. Common sandpiper breed on many of the lower stretches and the shy heron, brilliant blue kingfisher and white bibbed dipper are occasionally seen. The Derwent in Forge Valley, the Rye near Rievaulx, and streams in Dalby Forest are especially good places to watch the wildlife of rivers.

The Farndale daffodils – a spectacle of the moors in spring.

In early spring a riverside walk in Farndale is one of the high points of the moorland year. Wild daffodils flower profusely along the banks of the River Dove. Possibly planted by monks, they are protected by by-laws in Farndale local nature reserve.

Sutton Bank nature trail winds through dense oak woodland to Lake Gormire at the foot of Whitestone Cliff.

Wild flowers have been disappearing from the British countryside at a phenomenal rate. Ninety-five per cent of all flower-rich haymeadows and pastures have been converted to reseeded grass fields or ploughed up and drained for arable cultivation since the War. There is now little left, and the North York Moors is no exception. Only a few fragments survive, where globe flower, birds-eye primrose, marsh helleborine, orchids and the insectivorous butterwort cling on. Old quarry workings provide a haven for dry grassland species, though these become threatened when the hollows are used as tips.

Cowslip.

In many districts once widespread plants are now relegated to the roadside verge. To focus attention on their importance during 1985, two local naturalists, Margaret Atherden and Nan Sykes, undertook a comprehensive survey of the entire 1,000 miles of roadside verge in the national park – about three per cent of its total area. The verges were monitored in early spring, and early and late summer, on foot, by bicycle and from a slow-moving car. Their research revealed upwards of 440 different species – over half the total number in the national park, including several rare orchids.

With the changing season cowslip, primrose and violet give way to displays of sweet cicely, cow parsley, stitchwort and red campion followed by the yellows of bird's-foot trefoil and hawkweeds – all a

Common blue. A butterfly of agriculturally unimproved grassland and roadside verges.

vital and colourful part of enjoying the countryside. The variety of wild flowers brings an abundance of butterflies – common blue, small copper, meadow brown, ringlet, small tortoiseshell, peacock and skipper dancing over the roadside vegetation. At night moths are picked out in the car headlights.

A wealth of plants, their seeds and insects attract small birds, such as dunnock, yellowhammer, goldfinch and linnet, as well as mice, voles, and shrews. In turn these are hunted by birds of prey and carnivorous mammals. Kestrel, tawny, little and barn owls all hunt the roadside verge as do stoats and weasels.

Abused, dug up, parked on, mowed too little or too much, used as a dumping ground and a holding place for straw bales: it is increasingly clear that we would all do well to treat the roadside verge with a great deal more respect.

# 12 In and around the national park

Reponsibility for administration of the national park and furthering the aims of conservation and enjoyment lies with the North York Moors National Park Committee, a committee of North Yorkshire County Council. Comprising representatives of North Yorkshire County Council, Cleveland County Council and local district councils, along with nominees of the Secretary of State for the Environment, its day-to-day working is undertaken by a widely skilled professional staff centred on Helmsley.

Each year an estimated eleven million visits are made to the moors. To cater for demand the Authority developed an Information Service producing an extensive series of publications, including an annual *Visitor* newspaper. In 1976 it converted Danby Lodge, an old shooting lodge, into 'The Moors Centre', with exhibitions, indoor and outdoor activities, bookshop, cafeteria and a Youth and Schools Liaison Service. At Sutton

The Moors Centre, Danby Lodge, in Eskdale.

Bank a purpose-built centre, housing an exhibition and bookshop, provides a 'first stop' for visitors using this major gateway to the park.

Rangers, a mainstay and the 'public face' of the National Park Authority, are on hand to assist the public, as well as undertake many land management tasks. With expert knowledge of the region they are an important back-up for fire, police and ambulance personnel in emergencies. A regular published programme of 'Walks with a Ranger' is undertaken each year from numerous locations.

Most people travel to the moors by car. Public transport is largely limited to through routes within the moors, though the Committee has a policy to encourage rural services. Financial assistance has been given to bus companies running special summer 'Moorsbus' services at weekends and bank holidays from Middlesbrough and York, linking the Moors Centre at Danby, Lastingham and Hutton-le-Hole with urban areas. Normal service buses operate on many through routes and British Rail's Middlesbrough to Whitby line serves several villages along the Esk Valley. At Middlesbrough, services to Darlington connect with inter-city trains. Scheduled flights into Teesside airport link with rail connections into the park.

Over 1,100 miles of footpaths offer wide opportunities for visitors to weave their own way through hills and dales. The Cleveland Way long-distance footpath is an ideal route for more energetic walkers. Starting near Helmsley it curves ninety miles via Sutton Bank, Saltburn, Whitby and Robin Hood's Bay to Filey. In the past the forty-two mile Osmotherley to Ravenscar, Lyke Wake Walk was popular, but recently many people have refrained from using it following requests to relieve pressure which had caused severe erosion. Details of 'Waymarked Walks', published by the National Park Authority, are available from information centres and many shops. These outline a wealth of ideas for enjoying and understanding different areas of the moors. For example, ten linked stages make up the Esk Valley walk. Following the railway it enables the visitor to walk one way, returning by train. Especially popular are routes through woodland and along waterside places leading to waterfalls such as Mallyan Spout near Goathland, and Falling Foss, Littlebeck. Many woodland walks begin in Dalby Forest where the eight-mile Dalby Forest Drive (a toll road) winds through extensive conifer plantations. A comprehensive walks leaflet

Walkers on the Esk
Valley walk enjoy a rest.

is available from the Forestry Commission's Dalby
Forest information centre. 'Moorsrail' steam and
diesel services running between Pickering and
Grosmont all stop at Newtondale Halt. From here
remote areas of woodland, enhanced by dramatic
glacial scenery, are easily accessible.

Pony trekking is popular, and many centres cater
for holidays or shorter hire. Fishing is available on
several rivers, sailing at Scaling Dam, rowing and
canoeing at Ruswarp on the Esk and gliding and
hang-gliding takes place at Carlton and Sutton
Banks.

Famous historical characters are an important
part of the cultural heritage of any region. Despite
the relative insignificance of the coast in the
moorland story, it was the sea and global
exploration from which the moors inherited its best
known son. The Captain James Cook Heritage Trail
traces the haunts of this world-famous mariner and
explorer. From Marton, near Middlesbrough,
where Cook was born in 1724 it takes in Airyholme
Farm, his home as a boy; Cook Schoolhouse
Museum, Great Ayton; Staithes where he was
apprenticed to a haberdasher and grocer's
merchant; Whitby where the *Endeavour* was built
and Cook Monument, erected to his memory on
Easby Moor in 1827.

Laurence Sterne, rector of Coxwold and said by
some to be the father of the English novel, came to

live at Shandy Hall, an Elizabethan house in the village, where he wrote *Life and Times of Tristram Shandy, Gentleman* and *Sentimental Journey*. Barely recognized in this country, Sterne has a considerable following overseas, especially in the United States.

Traditional Yorkshire coble fishing boats at Staithes.

Far more widely known is the late Robert Thompson, wood carver of Kilburn. A mouse symbol trademark carved into his oak furniture, earned him the nickname 'The Mouseman'. Kilburn is also famous for a somewhat larger animal. In 1857, the local schoolmaster and thirty helpers cut a 314 ft (95 m) long by 228 ft (69 m) high horse in the face of Roulston Scar above the village. Visible from considerable distances, the white horse is in reality more of a dirty grey – the colour of the underlying rock. Only a coat of chalk brightens its colours.

In addition to large Forestry Commission caravan and camp sites at May Beck and Spiers House, Cropton Forest, private facilities are widespread. Also in Cropton Forest at Keldy Castle wooden Scandinavian cabins are popular, and bookings need to be made well in advance. Nine Youth Hostels, including the 'WHO' – Westerdale, Helmsley and Osmotherley – provide low-cost accommodation.

Esk Valley and Little
Fryup Dale from Oakley
Walls.

The North York Moors is the driest national park
in England and Wales. It is often quite windy on the
moortops, though sheltered in the dales. Spring
comes late and snow flurries are not uncommon into
May. Sometimes thick mist and cloud envelope the
hills and care needs to be taken not to stray from the
path when walking and to wear suitable clothing in
poor weather conditions.

Each season brings new character to the
landscape, from deep purples of heather in summer
and fiery orange of bracken in autumn, to miles of
brilliant smooth and undulating snows of winter.
Although winter visits can be breathtaking, caution
and wisdom are necessary to ensure roads are clear
and the weather settled before setting out.

Water has a magnetic attraction. However, in
spite of a long and impressive coastline, the shore is
relatively inaccessible. Sandsend and Runswick Bay
have the best sandy beaches. At Whitby, in
midsummer, it is possible to watch the sun set over
the sea, even though you are in the east of England.
Boggle Hole, Saltwick Bay, Hayburn and Cloughton
Wykes and the fishing villages of Staithes, where
some older women still wear traditional cotton
bonnets, and Robin Hood's Bay, with its narrow
alleys and tightly packed houses, are very popular.
In recognition of the outstanding scenery, the
Countryside Commission defined the entire national
park coast, along with an adjacent stretch in
Cleveland, as a heritage coast in 1974.

Inland, numerous bridge or ford crossings of
streams are ideal spots to find an isolated picnic
place beside water. A stream running through the
midst of Hutton-le-Hole and the River Esk in

Kilburn white horse.

Lealholm make these two of the most attractive villages in the park.

Stunning views and wide vistas are the very essence of the moors. Many are easily reached by car, though yet more remain the province of those prepared to walk a little way. Selected views, suitable for car passenger or walker are noted in 'Selected places of interest'.

On the assumption that the millions of visitors each year cast a 'vote with their feet', there is overwhelming support for conservation of the fine moorland landscape. Indeed, the principal reason for the national park designation in 1952 was to protect the heather moorland; yet since then one quarter of the moorland area has disappeared under conifer forest and upland pasture. The conservation of this moorland is essential if we are to retain the character of the region and especially the wild life, for which it is a 'last home'. Insidious encroachment by bracken also plays an increasing part and devastation by accidental fires has seriously damaged other large areas. In the hot dry summer of 1976, fires, probably started by dropped cigarettes, totally burned out vast sections of Wheeldale and Glaisdale Moors, leaving a grey, stony, lunar landscape where little can be expected to grow for many years.

How can so much have gone and why has it been allowed to disappear? The Forestry Commission cannot really be blamed; it had a statutory duty to plant trees on land which it had already purchased. Nor can farmers, for they only sought to make the best living possible in often difficult circumstances – something agricultural incentives were designed to help them do. Neither is it the fault of the National Park Authority; it has done everything within its powers and financial limitations to minimize the effects of other national policies pulling in different directions, by extensive consultation on proposed new schemes, management agreements with farmers and even outright purchase of major areas such as Lockton High and Levisham Moors to protect them from unwelcome change.

The blame for what can only be described as inadequate policies for the integration of landscape and wildlife conservation, agriculture, forestry and recreation, lies firmly at the feet of successive governments. In practice they have singularly failed to give national parks any real statutory meaning or protection or adequate funding for the Authorities to carry out their immensely difficult task.

In a recent North York Moors National Park Annual Report Martin Territt, the Chairman, explained the challenges which his Committee faces:

> 'Although the public concern for the protection of the environment has never been greater, it is surprising that in the 1980s, a body like a National Park Committee has to resort to the purchase of land to prevent damaging operations. That my Committee decided to do this at Lockton, in an unfavourable financial climate, illustrates our resolve to conserve the North York Moors.'

In a largely privately owned landscape, it is never likely to be a simple task! Nevertheless many of the problems generated by the lack of a cohesive and properly funded strategy by central government are being tackled with imagination within the limited resources available to the park. At present, at least eight grant-aid schemes covering farm conservation, woodland management, tree planting, wildlife conservation and village improvement, amongst others, are available to help protect and enhance the qualities of the landscape.

If new financial incentives and government policies which draw agriculture, forestry and park objectives together are forthcoming, then there is a good chance that co-operation and goodwill can solve the conservation conflicts. But nature may ultimately have a final say: bracken is spreading at the rate of over 300 acres per year. Through interpretation of the latest satellite imagery from space, the scale of the potential problem has become abundantly clear. Over two-thirds of the

Bracken is creeping on to the heather moor at a rate of over 300 acres each year.

heather moorland is vulnerable to encroachment.

The more bracken, the less heather; the less heather then the lower the value of grazing and grouse shooting. Less income from sheep and grouse means less management of the moors, which leads to more bracken and an increased risk of conversion to forestry or pasture, with a loss of vital wildlife habitat either way. It is a vicious circle which the National Park Authority, through its Moorland Management Programme, is in the best position to break.

Loss of the heather moorland also means loss of all the wildlife living there.

# Selected places of interest

The numbers after each place-name are the map grid references to help readers locate the places mentioned. Ordnance Survey maps include instructions on the use of these grid references.

AMPLEFORTH (SE 583787) Home of modern Roman Catholic monastery and Ampleforth College public school. The Abbey church is open to the public.

APPLETON-LE-MOORS (SE 735878) Good example of a single-street village of traditional houses with parallel back lanes, tofts and crofts and a common.

BOTTON HALL (NZ 696041) Two miles south of Castleton in Danby Dale. Steiner Foundation community offering a place in society for the adult mentally handicapped: coffee bar, gift shop and craft bakery, and creamery products available.

COXWOLD (SE 535772) Interesting village of traditional houses. Church has an unusual octagonal tower. Laurence Sterne, the famous novelist and rector of Coxwold, lived at Shandy Hall from 1760 to 1768. Nearby, the twelfth-century Byland Abbey is noted for its fine glazed tiles, beautifully shaped ruins and gateway straddling the Oldstead road.

DALBY FOREST DRIVE (SE 848855 to SE 909910) Eight-mile drive (tollroad) through the heart of the Forestry Commission's Dalby Forest with picnic places, trails and information centre. At the east end Bickley Forest garden displays specimens of every different tree to be found in the forest.

GOATHLAND (NZ 835013) A green jewel amongst the dark moorland. Wide village greens, grazed by free-roaming sheep; Mallyan Spout waterfall and 'Moorsrail' (the North York Moors historic railway) station make this isolated village a popular resort in summer.

GROSMONT (NZ 830053) Northern terminus of Moorsrail, and junction with British Rail Esk Valley, Middlesbrough to Whitby line. Centre for nineteenth-century iron mining. The Historical Railway Trail links it with Beck Hole and Goathland. Locomotive sheds open to the public.

GUISBOROUGH (NZ 610160) Ancient capital of Cleveland. Ruined twelfth-century Augustinian priory; working water-mill one mile east on A173. Market held in wide cobble-fringed street on Mondays and Saturdays.

HELMSLEY (SE 612838) South-west gateway to the moors. A market town – market day Friday – with ancient cross in square. National Park headquarters based in the Old Vicarage. Duncombe Park with parkland, formal gardens and temple adjoins the town south of the ruined castle.

HUTTON-LE-HOLE (SE 705900) Popular village of traditional houses centred around stream and wide sheep-grazed greens.

KIRKBYMOORSIDE (SE 698863) Quiet small market town with sixteenth-century public house, the Black Swan. Market held each Wednesday.

LADY CHAPEL (SE 454982) Sixteenth-century chapel one mile north west of Osmotherley. Fine views over Vale of York.

NEWBURGH PRIORY (SE 542765) One mile south of Coxwold. Seventeenth and eighteenth-century house with fine frontage, wild water garden and roadside lake. Oliver Cromwell's remains are reputed to lie here.

NUNNINGTON HALL (SE 670795) Four and a half miles south east of Helmsley. Sixteenth-century manor house. Home of Carlisle collection of miniature rooms. A National Trust property.

PICKERING (SE 796841) Ideal springboard for enjoying the national park with ruined medieval castle and important religious wall paintings in parish church. Southern terminus of the eighteen-mile Moorsrail. Market day is Monday.

RIEVAULX TERRACES AND TEMPLES (SE 579847) Two and a half miles north west of Helmsley. A half-mile long curved grass terrace set amongst deciduous woodland with classical style temples at either end. Offers several magnificent, romantic views over Rievaulx Abbey.

ROBIN HOOD'S BAY (NZ 952050) Known locally as 'Bay' or 'Bay town', the delightful tightly packed houses and narrow alleyways enhance the coastal character of a village huddled against the sea. In the past houses sometimes fell into the sea until a new sea wall stemmed cliff erosion. Marner Dale, a nature reserve, fills the small valley behind the village.

ROSEDALE ABBEY (SE 724960) Boom town of the nineteenth-century iron-mining era. Extensive industrial archaeological features abound in the surrounding dale. The sparse remains of a twelfth-century nunnery are built into the parish church.

SANDSEND (NZ 860128) One of many centres for eighteenth-century alum working. Renowned for its long sandy beach.

STAITHES (NZ 782188) Picturesque fishing village wedged into the coastal cliffs in the mouth of Roxby Beck. Captain Cook's cottage stands near the sea wall.

THORNTON DALE (SE 834830) Busy, attractive village, with ancient cross and stocks. Some houses have small bridges to cross roadside streams. Gateway to Dalby Forest to the north east.

# Exceptional views

'C' denotes places which can be reached directly by car.

BAXTERS'S VIEW – C (SE 943889) 4 m N of Wykeham

BIRK BROW – C (NZ 659149) 3 m E of Guisborough

BLAKEY RIGG – C (SE 685988) 6 m S of Castleton

BLUE BANK – (NZ 868059) 1 m S of Sleights

COOK MONUMENT/EASBY MOOR (NZ 590101) 2 m SE of Great Ayton

CROSSCLIFF VIEWPOINT (SE 895916) 4 m NE of Low Dalby

DANBY BEACON – C (NZ 737093) 2 m NE of the Moors Centre, Danby

HASTY BANK – C (NZ 573036) 4 m SE of Stokesley

HOLE OF HORCUM – C (SE 853938) 6 m N of Thornton Dale

KILBURN WHITE HORSE (SE 514813) 7 m W of Helmsley

NEWGATE BANK – C (SE 564890) 4 m NW of Helmsley

PEAK SCAR VIEWPOINT – C (SE 526884) 3 m NE of Boltby

RAVENSCAR – C (NZ 980020)

REASTY BANK – C (NZ 966945) 2 m N of Hackness

ROSEBERRY TOPPING (NZ 579127) 2 m NE of Great Ayton

ROSEDALE CHIMNEY BANK – C (SE 720946) 1 m S of Rosedale Abbey

ROSEDALE HEAD – C (NZ 679020) 4 m S of Castleton

SURPRISE VIEW – C (SE 684901) E end of Gillamoor village

SUTTON BANK – C (SE 514829) 7 m W of Helmsley

WAINSTONES (NZ 557036) 4 m SE of Stokesley

# Information centres

THE MOORS CENTRE – The National Park Visitor Centre (NZ 715084) – $\frac{1}{2}$m E of Danby. Special facilities available for school study groups. Tel: Castleton (0287) 60654

SUTTON BANK – National Park Information Centre (SE 514829) – 5 m E of Thirsk. Tel: Thirsk (0845) 597426

DALBY FOREST – Forestry Commission (SE 856874) – 3 m N of Thornton Dale. Tel: Pickering (0751) 60295

PICKERING STATION – North York Moors railway (SE 797842) – centre of Pickering. Tel: Pickering (0751) 73791

RAVENSCAR – National Trust (NZ 979016) – clifftop near Raven Hall Hotel

RYEDALE FOLK MUSEUM (SE 705900) – Hutton-le-Hole. Tel: Lastingham (07515) 367

# Museums

BECK ISLE MUSEUM OF RURAL LIFE – Pickering (SE 795842)

COOK BIRTHPLACE MUSEUM – Stewarts Park, Marton (NZ 516162) 6 m W of Guisborough

COOK SCHOOLHOUSE MUSEUM – Great Ayton (NZ 561107)

RYEDALE FOLK MUSEUM – Hutton-le-Hole (SE 705900)

SHANDY HALL/Laurence Sterne Collection – Coxwold (SE 532774)

WOOD END MUSEUM (natural history) – Scarborough

ROTUNDA (Archaeology) – Scarborough

CRESCENT ART GALLERY – Scarborough

PANNETT PARK MUSEUM AND ART GALLERY – Whitby (NZ 894109)

Note: Many information centres and places of interest are open daily throughout the summer season. However some have irregular opening times and one or two are restricted to a single day each week. You are advised to check if planning a special visit.

# Bibliography | Useful addresses

The North York Moors National Park Department publishes a wide range of leaflets and booklets about the moors. Those of particular interest to the visitor include:

**Newspaper**
*The Visitor*

**Leaflets**
*Waymarked Walk leaflets* – over 30 suggested routes to suit the family

**Booklets**
*Esk Valley Walk*
*Hambleton Drove Road*
*Heritage Coast/Sandsend Trail*
*Historical Railway Trail*
*Geology of the North York Moors*
*May Beck Trail*
*Ravenscar Geological Trail*
*Spout House*
*Sutton Bank Trail*

**Books**
*History of Hutton-le-Hole*
*History of Rosedale*

National park publications are available from the national park information centres as well as many other local shops or direct from the park's Information Officer in Helmsley, who can also supply a full list of publications.

**Other reading**
Atkinson, J C *Countryman on the Moors* (ed. J G O'Leary), Oxford University Press, 1983.
Hartley, M and Ingilby, J *Life in the Moorlands of North-East Yorkshire*, Dent, 1972.
Mead, H *Inside the North York Moors*, David and Charles, 1978.
Morris, R W *Yorkshire Through Place Names*, David and Charles, 1982.

North York Moors
National Park Department
The Old Vicarage
Bondgate
Helmsley YO6 5BP
(Tel: Helmsley (0439) 70657)

Cleveland Nature Conservation Trust
The Old Town Hall
Mandale Road
Thornaby
Stockton-on-Tees
Cleveland
(Tel: Stockton-on-Tees (0642) 608405)

Countryside Commission
Yorkshire and Humberside Regional Office
8a Otley Road
Headingley
Leeds LS6 2AD
(Tel: Leeds (0532) 742935)

Forestry Commission
43 Eastgate
Pickering
(Tel: Pickering (0751) 73810)

National Trust
27 Tadcaster Road
York
(Tel: York (0904) 702021)

Nature Conservancy Council
Matmer House
Hull Road
York
(Tel: York (0904) 412420)

Yorkshire Wildlife Trust
10 Toft Green
York
(Tel: York (0904) 59570)

# Index

Page numbers in *italics* refer to illustrations.